THE BELFAST & COUNTY DOWN RAILWAY

An Irish Railway Pictorial

Desmond Coakham

Midland Publishing Limited

The Belfast & County Down Railway
© 1998 Desmond Coakham

ISBN 1 85780 076 1

Published by
Midland Publishing Limited
24 The Hollow, Earl Shilton
Leicester, LE9 7NA, England.
Tel: 01455 847 815 Fax: 01455 841 805
E-mail: midlandbooks@compuserve.com

Design concept and layout
© Midland Publishing Limited
and Stephen Thompson Associates.

Printed in England by
Woolnough Bookbinding Limited
Irthlingborough, Northamptonshire.

Front cover photograph: **The only surviving
BCDR locomotive is 4-4-2 tank No 30,
which is currently on display at the Ulster
Folk & Transport Museum at Cultra. The
museum building is actually connected by
a spur to the only surviving BCDR line, the
branch to Bangor. Here No 30 makes a
stirring sight as she steams out of Queen's
Quay on 17th April 1948.** H C Casserley

Title page: **The former BCDR 4-4-2T No 20,
now renumbered 220 by its new owners, the
Ulster Transport Authority, heads a down
Bangor train out of Carnalea on 14th May
1950. This was the year of infamy in which
the rest of the BCDR was prematurely
closed down by the UTA.** H C Casserley

CONTENTS

INTRODUCTION
AND HISTORICAL SKETCH

*A large part of the 'County Down'
goes from a small part of County Down.*

That was the cumbersome headline to greet
Northern Whig readers on the 16th January
1950, the day following closure of the Belfast &
County Down Railway's main line, or at least
that portion of it from Comber Junction to its
seaside terminus at Newcastle. The Ballynahinch
and Ardglass branches had closed two days
before and a further section from Ballymacarrett
Junction to Donaghadee would go in a matter
of weeks. The *Whig*, long since as extinct as the
BCDR, was addicted to punning headlines, but
this one gave the impression that the event,
first fruits of public ownership of rail transport
in Northern Ireland, was being played down.
In fact we were witnessing the beginnings of a
process that would lead to the destruction of
most of Ulster's railways and which culminated
in the closure of the trunk railway from
Portadown to Londonderry and the abandon-
ment of rail freight in the province, in 1965.

The Belfast & County Down Railway was a
child of the 1846 'Railway Mania'. Opening its
four-mile long Holywood branch on 2nd
August 1848, and the first portion of main line,
the 12 miles to Newtownards via Comber on
6th May 1850, it took nine more years and
another Act of Parliament to reach its intended
goal of Downpatrick. Services to the county
town of Down, 27 miles by rail from Belfast,
began on 23rd March 1859. Its gauge was
5ft 3in, the Irish standard.

The original Act had allowed for a more or
less direct line from Comber to Downpatrick.
Delay in obtaining sufficient funds gave time
for further consideration. A shift westward put
the villages of Saintfield and Crossgar on the
route, with the market town of Ballynahinch
accessible by a branch of only 3½ miles long.
Here, ulterior motives may be discerned.
Ballynahinch would have been a staging post
on the grandiose 'Short Sea Passage British &
Irish Union' project where the County Down
company was to build a line linking it to the
Dublin & Belfast Junction Railway, to create a
through route between the Irish capital and
Scotland via the port of Donaghadee. The
D&BJR was also offered land at the BCDR
Belfast Terminus for its own station, freeing it
from dependence on the Ulster Railway for
access to Belfast. But the Ulster company was
very much the senior railway out of Belfast and
soon put paid to BCDR ambitions. Laid out as a
through station of the line to Banbridge and
the south, Ballynahinch remained a terminus
for its whole existence. It was 21 miles from
Belfast by rail, but a mere 14 miles by road.
From its opening day on 10th September 1858
there was immediate competition from omnibus proprietors and carriers, all of whom had
to be bought out.

The County Down directors of that crucial
period appeared hellbent on laying up trouble
for their successors. Newtownards, the most
important town in North Down, was only nine
miles by road from Belfast and rail fares had to
take that into account. Now the line was to be
extended from Comber to Newtownards and
Donaghadee, making the distance from Belfast
to the little seaport unnecessarily long at 22
miles. Additionally, provision was made for a
branch to Bangor harbour some 2½ miles in
length from Conlig on the Donaghadee line.
The two seaports had been contenders for the
harbour improvements the Admiralty was prepared to make in readiness for a steam-packet
service on the 'Short Sea Passage' to Portpatrick
in Galloway. As a result, the BCDR had to back
both horses by including railways to Bangor
and Donaghadee in its Act of 1846. These powers lapsed but were revived, though on differing
routes. In 1858 Donaghadee was proclaimed
the chosen port and its railway was opened on
3rd June 1861, thus the Bangor branch was
abandoned, even though much property in the
town centre had already been purchased.

The County Down had staked a lot on Government promises. Donaghadee harbour was
duly improved, but public money was spent to
no avail on Portpatrick harbour, which remained
little more than a cove on an inhospitable
coastline and the mail packet service never
materialised. The BCDR was now deeply in
debt. The modest dividends paid in the 1850s
were wiped out, and a 35-year Government
loan of £160,000 (roughly the amount of the
company's borrowing powers) at 3½% did little
to cushion the years of poverty that lay ahead.

Perhaps the unkindest cut of all came from
the BCDR's Scottish ally, for the Portpatrick
Railway, *en route* to its eponymous terminus,
continued on to Stranraer at the head of Loch
Ryan. The temptation offered by this safe, land-
locked harbour was too much. Stranraer
became, and still is, the port for the Irish traffic.
No time was wasted on promoting a railway
from the Belfast & Northern Counties' railhead
at Carrickfergus to Larne Harbour in County
Antrim, and an associated steamer service
between Stranraer and Larne commenced on
2nd October 1862.

During preparations for the Donaghadee
extension in 1857, realisation began to dawn
on the County Down board that the most
obvious route for a Belfast to Bangor railway
was by extending the Holywood branch. As the
BCDR had exhausted its own resources, the
eight mile line was undertaken by an assem-
blage of local notables. The Belfast, Holywood
& Bangor Railway was incorporated in 1860
and took five years to complete, having almost
immediately fallen into the hands of the
London Financial Association, a situation
shared with a number of other small railways in
the United Kingdom. The Holywood Company,
as it was commonly referred to in BCDR corre-
spondence, was empowered to make agree-
ments with the BCDR for the latter to work the
BHBR and to supply engines and rolling stock.

The ink was hardly dry on the working agreement when the BCDR was beguiled into a bolder course of action, the lease of its most profitable section, the Holywood branch, to the BHBR for a downpayment of £50,000 cash and a yearly rent of £5,000. There was apprehension from some shareholders, but the lure of ready money was too great for their directors. The Transfer Act was secured shortly after the BHBR opened to Bangor on 18th May 1865. Provisions included the handing-over of a sizeable portion of the Belfast terminus and the transfer of BCDR staff employed on the Holywood line. Transition was relatively easy as the branch had been operated independently of the main line from its earliest days. Ironically, the purchase money went straight into the coffers of the Northern Bank to reduce the BCDR overdraft.

There were great promises of improvement of the BHBR and provision for amenities in Bangor but, a year almost to the day from the line's opening all came to nothing when the failure of Overend & Gurney's Bank brought bankruptcy and ruin to the little railways of the London Financial Association's empire. Even so, the very presence of the railway brought steady growth to Bangor as a dormitory town and resort, and that growth was reflected in the increasing profitability of the BHBR, to the extent that the County Down Railway eventually received its arrears of rent.

Railway communication with the picturesque resort of Newcastle – where the Mourne Mountains swept down to the sea just as Percy French was to describe them in his famous ballad – was undertaken by the Downpatrick Dundrum & Newcastle Railway. The 11½ miles from a junction outside Downpatrick to a terminus on the northern outskirts of Newcastle presented few difficulties and the line opened

on 25th March 1869, having taken 16 months to build. The BCDR worked the line with its own stock. There were disagreements with the owners, but previous lessons had been learned and taken to heart.

The year 1875 marked the turning point in BCDR fortunes though much still had to be overcome. The outcome of the 'shareholders revolt' that August, introduces the first personality we have mentioned by name, the Dublin businessman Richard Woods Kelly, who became the BCDR chairman and remained in that position until his death in 1892. His period in office saw the transition from mediocrity to financial stability, and the new generation of executive officers who served his board rebuilt the old County Down infrastructure almost from scratch.

A formidable neighbour appeared in 1876. The Great Northern Railway of Ireland was an amalgamation of the Ulster Railway and its associated companies. A latent threat of attack from the west via the unfinished Banbridge Extension Railway was revived when the GNR purchased the line and in 1880 opened it to the hamlet of Ballyroney, where it remained an arrowhead aimed at the Downpatrick to Newcastle line. The BCDR did the sensible thing and purchased the DDNR in 1881 for £50,000.

During this period, the BCDR system was isolated from the rest of the Irish railway network. Its Belfast terminus was at Queen's Quay on the County Down side of the *River Lagan,* downstream from Queen's Bridge, while the Ulster and Belfast & Northern Counties stations lay across the river on the Country Antrim side of the city. Only the former UR terminus was within easy walking distance of the city centre. The Belfast Central Railway was incorporated in 1864 with the intention of linking

the Ulster Railway with the stations at Queen's Quay and the BNCR at York Road. It also hoped to build a central station that would be used by all the other companies. That was something which would take more than a century to accomplish.

Physical connection between the County Down lines and the rest of the network was not achieved until the complicated crossing of the Central Railway over BCDR and BHBR, a junction that had lain unfinished for years, was put into use on 12th May 1876. This was Ballymacarrett Junction, located in that part of the city which took its name from the legendary MacArt whose hillfort looked down from the Cave Hill away to the north, across Belfast Lough. The junction was half a mile from the Queen's Quay buffer-stops.

Below: **For many years, short workings from Queen's Quay to Holywood, extended occasionally to Craigswood at peak times, were a feature of the Bangor line. To avoid having to run the locomotive round its train these were worked on the push-pull principle. The locomotive was always at the Holywood end of the train. When it was pushing, the driver sat in the front of the leading coach, where he had a brake and other controls. The serious accident at Ballymacarrett Junction in January 1945 involved one of these trains. The smaller tank engines, such as No 7, seen here at Queen's Quay on 26th June 1937, were used on the Holywood push-pull workings. The white board on the buffer beam, rather than a lamp, was adopted by several Irish railways to denote the end of a train in daylight hours. H C Casserley**

Though there were many plans for them, no regular passenger services ran over the Lagan Viaduct and onto the County Down system. Plans for a central station were dropped, the three companies were content with their own termini. As built, the Belfast Central Railway proved useful for freight exchange and as a link with the dockside tramways of the Belfast Harbour Commissioners. It was snapped up by the Great Northern in 1885.

In 1884 the County Down Railway had finally gained the strength to absorb the BHBR, and from then, through the golden years to the First World War, never looked back. In 1885 the BCDR got an outstanding General Manager in Joseph Tatlow, recruited by Kelly from the Glasgow & South Western. His regime lasted less than six years, but public confidence was regained as stations and services were improved and decent carriages began to be provided. Further stimulation, affecting every railway in the Kingdom, was applied by the Regulation of Railways Act, 1889, itself a rapid parliamentary response to that year's Armagh disaster - continuous brakes for passenger trains, improved signalling and interlocking were the order of the day. Thanks to the BCDR Act of 1891, capital was flowing in to pay for all this. When Tatlow left the company in December 1890 to become Manager of the Midland Great Western Railway, he had laid the foundations for growth, which included the branch to Ardglass, sanctioned by the Downpatrick, Killough & Ardglass Light Railway Order in the previous September. This was one of the 'Baronially guaranteed' lines, built under the legislation designed to encourage railway construction in the less prosperous parts of Ireland. Interest on the capital used to construct such a line was guaranteed to be paid by

the ratepayers of the district it served, irrespective of whether the line was a success or not. The BCDR was allowed to build the Ardglass Railway by direct labour under the supervision of G P Culverwell, its Civil Engineer.

Culverwell had succeeded Berkley Wise in this post in 1888. Wise is famous for his work on the Northern Counties up to his premature death in 1906. On the BCDR from 1877, he had been the first engineer to seriously tackle the poor permanent way, and much of his energy was occupied in this direction, leaving him little chance to display the architectural talents that would later enhance the BNCR. His last undertaking on the County Down was the doubling of the main line from Ballymacarrett Junction to Knock.

The Ardglass branch opened for passenger traffic on 8th July 1892. It had a 'Harbour Tramway' through the streets to the port for the herring traffic but the line never lived up to expectations. In the prosperous years which lasted up to the end of the First World War, however, summer revenue usually cancelled out a loss on working in the winter months.

Concurrently with the construction of the Ardglass line, work began on a long awaited facility at Downpatrick, in the form of the Loop Line (see illustration below). This completed a triangle of lines and permitted through running for Newcastle trains, though the engaging practice of reversing trains at Downpatrick terminus was never abandoned. The Loop Line opened on 24th September 1892. The Loop Platform, in the 'V' of the South Junction that formed an interchange between the through Newcastle trains and Downpatrick Station, was added the following year. The Ardglass branch, diverging shortly beyond the South Junction, increased the Company's mileage by 8½.

The Loop Line as authorised was 26 chains (0.32 of a mile) long, but arranging the actual South Junction to suit the Loop platform lengthened it by 3 chains.

R W Kelly, who had gone abroad on medical advice in April 1891, was not able to enjoy these fruits of his chairmanship, dying in January 1892. The County Down Railway continued its programme of improvements, the years to 1902 seeing the doubling of the main line from Knock to Comber and the Bangor line.

The latter was done in stages from Holywood. Perhaps the most significant changes occurred at Newcastle. Tatlow had been eager to attract the golfing fraternity, and the BCDR subsidised what became the Royal County Down Golf Club by building its club house, the links being on the sandhills close to the station. There was free travel for golfers on its opening day. Then followed the boldest step, the construction of the Slieve Donard Hotel which had 100 bedrooms and all amenities, adjacent to the railway terminus. It cost around £56,000 and though it lost money to begin with, it became one of the company's best investments. The formal opening by the Countess Annesley took place on 21st June 1898, an apparent olive branch on the Earl's part, for the Annesley family, ruling the district in feudal fashion, were never friends of the BCDR, and there had been much trouble in purchasing land for the hotel.

The growing confidence of the BCDR was manifested the previous year when the Duke and Duchess of York were doing an Irish tour as part of Queen Victoria's 1897 Jubilee celebrations. Some very presentable royal trains were assembled by other companies, but County Down one-upmanship probably eclipsed all when a handsome clerestoried bogie saloon was purchased from the Ashbury Carriage & Iron Company of Manchester, costing upwards of £1,400.

The royal train made a return trip from Newtownards to Newcastle on 6th September 1897. The saloon, BCDR No 153, went under wraps in a heated carriage shed, to be used for the second time during the Coronation visit of King Edward VII and Queen Alexandra. By the 1920s, the directors realised that royalty was unlikely to holiday at County Down resorts again, and the lovely old vehicle became the 'Golfers' Saloon', making Saturdays only journeys to Newcastle. It is pleasing to report that the body shell of No 153, having miraculously survived for four decades in a field, is now in the hands of the Downpatrick Steam Railway, and it is devoutly to be hoped that this preservation body, will in due course, be able to provide a replica underframe and restore the coach, at least to its 'golfing' condition.

As the new century dawned, the threat of a GNR presence at Newcastle became a reality. The County Down was obliged in 1901 to obtain an Act to make a 3½ mile branch from Newcastle, (another reversal of direction for through trains), to meet the GNR end-on at Castlewellan.

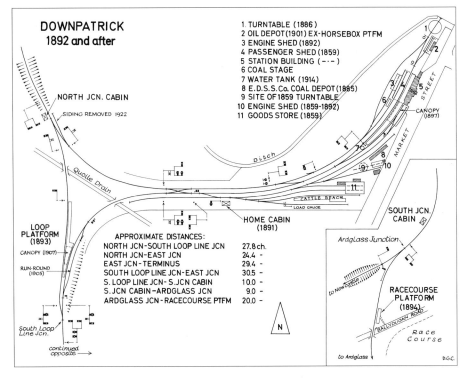

DOWNPATRICK
1892 and after

1. TURNTABLE (1886)
2. OIL DEPOT (1901) EX-HORSEBOX PTFM
3. ENGINE SHED (1892)
4. PASSENGER SHED (1859)
5. STATION BUILDING (-·-)
6. COAL STAGE
7. WATER TANK (1914)
8. E.D.S.S.Co. COAL DEPOT (1885)
9. SITE OF 1859 TURNTABLE
10. ENGINE SHED (1859-1892)
11. GOODS STORE (1859)

NORTH JCN. CABIN
SIDING REMOVED 1922
CANOPY (1897)

LOOP PLATFORM (1893)
CANOPY (1907)
RUN-ROUND (1905)

South Loop Line Jcn.

continued opposite →

Quoile Drain

Ditch

APPROXIMATE DISTANCES:
NORTH JCN-SOUTH LOOP LINE JCN   27.8 ch.
NORTH JCN-EAST JCN   24.4 -
EAST JCN-TERMINUS   29.4 -
SOUTH LOOP LINE JCN-EAST JCN   30.5 -
S. LOOP LINE JCN- S. JCN CABIN   10.0 -
S. JCN CABIN-ARDGLASS JCN   9.0 -
ARDGLASS JCN-RACECOURSE PTFM   20.0 -

HOME CABIN (1891)
CATTLE BEACH
LOAD GAUGE

SOUTH JCN. CABIN

Ardglass Junction

to Newcastle

RACECOURSE PLATFORM (1894)
BALLYDUGAN ROAD
Race Course

N

to Ardglass

D.G.C.

Above: **Though the County Down was a railway where passenger traffic was more important than the conveyance of goods, the proximity of Queen's Quay to the wharves and docks on the *River Lagan* meant that the Company's sole 0-6-4 shunting tank, No 29, was kept busy working trains along the quayside tramways of the Belfast Harbour Commissioners. On 24th June 1938 No 29 has just arrived in the goods yard at Queen's Quay with a train of locomotive coal from the quays. The east end of Queen's Quay shed is behind the locomotive.** H C Casserley

There was a strange delay on the latter company's part in making the extension, the first GNR trains steaming into Newcastle on 24th March 1906. The terminus had been given a badly needed facelift, and the BCDR was rewarded with reciprocal running powers to Ballyroney – useless, because the place had scarcely grown from 'six houses in the middle of a bog' – a description the Manager had given the BCDR board in 1879. The County Down gradually learned to live with its competitor at Newcastle. Greater GNR mileage from Belfast did little harm to BCDR passenger receipts and the resort benefited by having a direct route to Dublin and the south.

Ever since the dividing wall between the BCDR and BNBR stations came down in 1884, the city terminus had continued to expand, filling the long rectangle of land fronting on to Queen's Quay, and the goods yard, previously separated from the remainder of the BCDR facilities by the BHBR presence, was rationalised and enlarged. The old County Down running shed on the south side of the line became part of the combined locomotive, carriage and wagon shops, and the BHBR engine shed on the north side was incorporated into a new four-road 'through' shed. Goods trains now entered and left the yard by a connection at the outer end, controlled by the Ballymacarrett Junction cabin. Nearby, a two road shed was provided for the steam railcars introduced in 1904.

A long-term plan for a completely new station came to fruition in 1910, when work began on a new five-platform train shed. This was built on the site of the old passenger platforms while day-to-day operation went on at Queen's Quay. The original Company offices, facing Station Street, were extended at each end, with new lavatories and waiting rooms behind, these flanking one end of a large glazed-roof concourse. At the other end was the covered cab-rank and the terminal stub of Belfast Corporation's electric tramway, branching into Scrabo Street from the Queen's Road route and swinging into its arcade, where passengers might board and alight from the cars under cover. The new Queen's Quay terminus was largely complete by 1913, though no record of any special opening ceremony has been found.

Comparing the three Belfast termini, all of which have been razed to the ground within the last 30 years, one ventures the opinion that the remodelled Queen's Quay, built by the smallest company, was the best as far as practical considerations of passenger flow and convenience are concerned, though its siting on the 'wrong' side of the *Lagan* put it a poor second to the Great Northern terminus which was only a few minutes walk from the city centre.

The Northern Counties station at York Road had probably the best architecture of the three; a fine exterior by Sir Charles Lanyon, and a train shed which came close to rivalling that of the BCDR. Hitler's bombing in 1941 put paid to York Road's overall roof and most of the station frontage, while even in the last shabby years there was still a bit of style about the Queen's Quay train shed.

By August 1914, the BCDR was at its zenith, paying a 6½% dividend.

Other BCDR activities also deserve mention: the paddle steamer *Slieve Donard* in 1893 inaugurated a seasonal service between Bangor and a jetty at Donegall Quay, Belfast. The 'Bangor Boat' became a popular feature on Belfast Lough up to September 1915. The last and largest steamer was the *Erin's Isle* of 1912, requisitioned by the Admiralty in November 1915 and subsequently sunk by enemy action. Powers included in the BCDR Act of 1900 led to the establishment of road freight services between Newtownards and Portaferry and Newcastle and Kilkeel, using a variety of traction engines and steam wagons. The Kilkeel run proved to be the most useful, lasting from 1904 to 1925. The first BCDR motor omnibuses, again on a feeder service to Kilkeel, began running in August 1916.

BCDR officials took a pessimistic view of the Company's prospects when war broke out in August 1914. Some retrenchments were made but the volume of goods traffic remained unchanged, while passenger receipts increased quite dramatically in the first winter of the war. The enlarged military camp at Ballykinlar was given an unadvertised halt in late 1915, but little else was recorded before a curtain of censorship came down. Government control was imposed on the Irish railways in 1916, the Irish Railway Executive Committee remaining in office until 1st January 1920. Traffic was brisk in the post-war boom years but arrears of maintenance had accumulated in all departments. When materials became available the BCDR embarked on a comprehensive programme of bridge replacement, culminating in the complete renewal of its biggest engineering work, the Quoile Viaduct at Downpatrick, which was finished in 1929.

Most fortunately, between 1920 and 1924, a programme of motive power renewal was carried through, before the money ran out. Twelve new steam locomotives were obtained, representing a replacement of more than a third of the total stock. As a consequence, the County Down was still in remarkably good shape by the time the Second World War began, when it was to be tested to its limit.

Meanwhile, there were two decades of bitter competition to endure. After the Great War there was unregulated competition from bus operators. The effect was felt most keenly on the main line and its branches, where the discrepancy between distances by rail and road from Belfast to the important towns and villages was all too obvious. That the BCDR was able to fight back to the extent it did was largely due to its last General Manager, the redoubtable W F Minnis. Once a boy clerk on the County Down Railway, he achieved high office in 1926. 'Billy' Minnis was not afraid of fare-cutting and many bargain excursion tickets became available, including 'Bangor and Back for a Bob' – a slogan which has passed into folk-

lore. One notable enterprise operated annually from 1928 to 1936. This was in conjunction with the 'Round the Houses' motor race, the Ulster Tourist Trophy event which by its very nature severed road communication between Dundonald, Comber and Newtownards as well as the BCDR Donaghadee branch.

The County Down turned the races to its advantage by providing grandstands at strategic points (with refreshments!) and shuttle trains either side of the level crossing outside Comber, where temporary wooden platforms were available and a timber footbridge spanned the course. In September 1936 several spectators were killed in Newtownards when a racing car mounted the pavement, and the 'Round the Houses' race was never staged again.

The 1933 railway strike in Northern Ireland was a ruinous affair leading to the withdrawal of passenger services from several branch lines. On the County Down however, the men very wisely refused to strike, knowing that it would be the final nail in the coffin. Two diesel-electric locomotives for branch line use were obtained in the 1930s. As this mode of traction was in the pioneering stage, both units suffered a lot of mechanical trouble, but when they were in service the resulting economies were quite striking.

The BCDR was able to counter some of the omnibus competition by putting its own buses on the roads, notably between Holywood and Belfast, where the motor-trains had been badly hit, and a feeder service into Donaghadee from villages on the Ards peninsula. The larger railways had gone into bus and lorry operation

with a good deal of success, but all including the BCDR were to lose their road services in 1935 to the state-sponsored Northern Ireland Road Transport Board, which concentrated all opposing passenger and freight activities into a competitive monopoly. The railways surrendered their road vehicles in return for worthless stock in the new undertaking. There was also a highly suspect traffic-pooling arrangement. Scarcely any overall profit was made by the NIRTB, the freight department losing money up to 1941 and consistently after the Second World War. Many will recall the sight of an NIRTB freight shed in every provincial goods yard of any importance, a monstrous parasite siphoning off the traffic, occupying ground obligingly provided by the railways.

Following the outbreak of war in September 1939, the Company's finances took a turn for the better, a profit being registered for the year 1940. Two serious air-raids on Belfast in Spring of 1941 had a dramatic effect on passenger

Below: **Although generally poor performers on the road, the four 4-6-4T Baltic tanks built by Beyer Peacock & Company Limited were most impressive to view and the pride of the BCDR locomotive fleet. Following the takeover of the BCDR in 1948, all four acquired the Ulster Transport Authority's black livery, complete with a crest on the cab. No 223 was recorded at Queen's Quay in August 1950, before working the 12.45pm departure to Bangor.** J G Dewing

receipts as many people found accommodation out of town. The entry of the United States into the war at the end of that year quickened the tempo, the province becoming a vast armed camp with troop movements by rail an everyday occurrence. Arrears of dividends began to be paid, and of more significance to the railway enthusiast, engines were overhauled and rebuilt – and fully painted and lined; no austerity on the County Down. Rolling stock also was fettled up and four bogie coaches were bought second-hand from the Northern Counties Committee of the London, Midland & Scottish Railway. A new locomotive was ordered from Beyer, Peacock & Company, it being delivered at the end of 1944.

Losses in the blitz were comparatively minor. One wagon, two carriages and an ancient camping coach were burnt out, along with the oil-gas plant that provided the means of lighting for most of the carriages. The Locomotive Engineer's office was also a victim and locomotive drawings and other records were destroyed. The same fate befell the works offices on the Northern Counties over in York Road, where the overall damage was much worse. Greater ill-fortune struck the BCDR on 10th January 1945, the day of the most serious accident in the Company's history, when 23 passengers were killed in a rear end collision at Ballymacarrett.

W F Minnis had retired as General Manager at the end of July 1944, to be succeeded by a 'committee of management' consisting of the senior officers of the Company. The Traffic Manager of the Great Northern Railway was appointed to a similar post on the BCDR. One of the GNR suburban railcars was tested successfully on the Bangor line and hints of an alliance between the two companies were seen. However, as soon as hostilities ceased, a further wave of competition was unleashed.

The BCDR management announced its intention to close all but the Bangor line in the face of mounting losses. The Stormont administration's solution was to amalgamate the BCDR with its deadly rival, the NIRTB. The sum of £485,990 was paid for the BCDR and on 1st October 1948 the new 'co-ordinated' road rail combine came into existence as the Ulster Transport Authority. Public opinion, moulded by the promise of modernisation, was generally favourable to the merger. Most of us were prepared to accept the loss of a couple of branches but thought the Newcastle line with its tourist potential was safe enough. To close the double road to Comber was unimaginable, for the post war building boom was already evident in Belfast's eastern suburbs. But the hidden agenda was quickly made manifest and the always profitable Bangor branch was the only survivor.

What makes an insignificant bygone railway so attractive to many people? It is a fascination that has long outlived the company inasmuch as many of its devotees are too young to have remembered it. It was both complete and compact, a perfect example of an Edwardian railway maintained in surprisingly good condition and yet maligned as slow and inefficient by its detractors. For the second time in its long existence, it had by the 1930s, become the butt of pantomime jokes. I commuted between Bangor and Belfast for 40 years, the early ones being a time when we had to sign the attendance book before a red line was drawn across it at 9.15am, and if a handful of 'lates' were recorded over a given period, we had to explain ourselves. The 8.35am up train seldom let us down. It was only after the severe winter of 1947 that such an explanation was demanded of the author, who rather enjoyed giving it. There were of course, occasional irritations. A three-hour evening journey to Bangor caused by the big 4-4-2 tank No 8 breaking a crank-axle on the 5.35pm express provided one's first experience of wrong line working, with a queue of down trains waiting to cross to the up road at Helen's Bay. But the aftermath of the Ballymacarrett collision was handled in exemplary fashion.

Leaving personal reminiscences aside, perhaps the County Down's greatest appeal was an aesthetic one, for the neat and uniform appearance of its steam engines was undeniable, with 28 out of 29 the products of Beyer, Peacock & Company Limited of Gorton, Manchester. Though they were divided among nine classes and six wheel arrangements (the seventh was the Sharp, Stewart rebuild, an 0-4-2T), the Beyer Peacock hallmarks stood out. It has been said that Beyers never built an ugly locomotive – it was surely the case on the BCDR.

It is time to mention the fourth member of the quartet of Victorian chief officers who shaped the BCDR. Robert George Miller, who served as Loco-motive Foreman (and later as Superintendent) from 1879 to 1919, was a London & North Western man who had been posted to Ireland as Locomotive Foreman to that company's satellite, the Dundalk Newry & Greenore Railway. He was a competent locomotive engineer but was consistently overruled on locomotive policy by directors who thought they knew better. Matters worsened on the appointment of G P Culverwell as Civil Engineer, on a higher salary. Culverwell was very conscious of his position as Company Engineer and of his Dublin University training. It was an echo of the even older medical situation of physician (gentleman) and of barber-surgeon (tradesman). Miller, who had much less interference when it came to rolling stock, put his stamp on the BCDR by initiating its 'house style' of square-cornered windows and panelling. It was first seen in his re-bodying of older BCDR and BHBR coaches, carried out with success in the 1880s. The oldest County Down carriage in 1948, first class saloon No 1, built in Queen's Quay shops in 1888, was of this style; Miller's later saloons had rounded corners to all mouldings.

The style may have been due to his association with the Worsdell brothers of the North Eastern Railway in England, both Crewe men in his time on the LNWR. From the early 1900s, all BCDR coaches save the rail-motors and the 1938 tri-composites were built at Queen's Quay. The limited space in its carriage shop dictated the continuing construction of 6-wheelers up to the 1920s.

Culverwell died in office shortly before Miller retired at the end of 1919 and was succeeded by his assistant, P A Arnott, who had been a North British man.

The new Locomotive Engineer (as the title now was), John L Crosthwait, had been the assistant Works Manager at Inchicore on the Great Southern & Western. Crosthwait inherited the four 'Baltic' tanks already under construction at Gorton, but chose a larger version of the 4-4-2 tank type when more engines were needed in 1923. Here again, the civil engineer had the last word.

The bridge renewal programme had been slowed down by the recession and Crosthwait was obliged to run Nos 8 and 16 with tanks only half-full. Arnott apparently forgot to notify the Locomotive Department when the work was done, the big tanks running thus for several years more than was necessary.

Like the other northern companies, the BCDR retained all three classes of passenger accommodation to the last. In a country where rules were made to be broken, this was an invitation to cheating and put an additional strain on Ticket Inspectors. The author recalls meeting an aggrieved customer, an otherwise respectable man who had plainly been caught himself, bitterly recounting how the Manager, whom he referred to as 'Ould Minnis', would personally examine tickets in second class compartments on busy summer Saturdays. The great popularity of second class on the BCDR was due to its attractive subscribers' rates; a monthly second class season ticket was cheaper than its equivalent in third class weeklies, while discounts on quarterly and yearly tickets were even greater. Ladies, and young people over school age and under 21 years got their season tickets at two-thirds the full rate. A first class yearly subscriber might also obtain tickets for wife and family at a moderate additional premium. The County Down had little to learn when it came to what would be called today, 'marketing'.

At the end of its independence, the BCDR handed over 206 coaching vehicles, including 9 passenger brakes, 4 bread vans (intended for the Ardglass fish traffic), 2 carriage trucks and 10 horseboxes. Of the 181 passenger carriages, only 22 were bogie vehicles; the remainder were 6-wheeled, and this provides some justification for unkind comments on the discomfort of travel on the County Down. Daily users of its trains soon found where the least uncomfortable seats were, it was wise to avoid the end compartments though unlike the competing NIRTB buses, the motion was still smooth enough for them to read their newspapers.

BCDR goods vehicles were conventional but distinctive. In former times, even the smaller railways built their own wagons, and the BCDR

Above: **On 14th May 1950, in a sylvan setting near Carnalea, 4-6-4T No 229 heads a down Bangor train consisting of eleven 6-wheelers through the pine trees of the Crawfordsburn Estate. The busy commuter line to Bangor is the only part of the BCDR system still in use today.** H C Casserley

was no exception, developing a tradition of home construction almost from the beginning. Contracts were placed with outside firms from time to time, especially in the boom years at the turn of the century, but from then until takeover, the Queen's Quay shops carried out their own programme of renewals, as funds permitted.

At the takeover by the UTA the wagon stock amounted to 629 revenue earning vehicles, the covered wagons being typically outside-framed. Several, classified 'goods and cattle' were of the traditional Irish pattern with steeply curved roofs and an open centre section, tarpaulin-sheeted. Open wagons were of 10- and 8-ton capacity, some of the latter with falling sides. There were also a handful of single-bolster timber wagons and 14 goods brake vans, totally enclosed.

Engineering needs were served by 23 ballast wagons, a ballast brake van and 9 rail wagons designed by J L Crosthwait – these ran coupled in threes to carry 45ft rails. Oddments included two gasholder trucks, a weighbridge fitters' van and a Locomotive Department breakdown van plus a small fleet of locomotive coal wagons, confined in their decrepitude to trips between Belfast Yard and the Abercorn Basin.

C Hamilton Ellis, the celebrated railway artist and historian, advanced the proposition that wherever one went, one found the appropriate train in the landscape. His theory was demolished by the march of state ownership and standardisation but it still held good in County Down before 1950. The Company's modest aims were perfectly reflected in its title, and the encompassing landscape of lush farmland, drumlins and distant mountains fitted those dark green engines and their crimson trains like a comfortable glove.

The Great Northern remained an incomer at Newcastle, though enlivening the scene for us by the contrast. Its trains were those of the Lagan Valley and the Upper Bann and had reached the coast by a stiff climb across a bleak watershed. The County Down made its winding way around the little hills, with no river valleys to follow. It was by no means an easy road, one of undulating gradients, some taxing like the long haul from Holywood to Craigavad, or the hard slog from Comber through the Gullet, that meanly-excavated trench through the whinstone, to Ballygowan.

One recalls a driver on the 'Golfers', as the Ballygowan tablet was snatched and we tore towards the Gullet, shouting above the roar of No 19's exhaust, 'this is where the big goods engines fall down on the job.' All three of these handsome locomotives, Nos 4, 10 and 14, were expected to take 46 wagons southwards from Comber without assistance. It was war-time, and the driver was very likely speaking from experience of abnormal loading. The footplate of the 'Golfers' was not the place for a protracted discussion, and the sights and sounds of the journey had put it out of mind by the time we reached Newcastle.

In the 48 years since closure, earthworks of the line that served the heart of County Down have, like the raths, forts and megaliths in the preceding five millenia of human occupation, merged imperceptively into the background. An airline passenger *en route* to Aldergrove Airport might look down to trace among the patchwork of fields the interrupted course of a sinuous green lane between overgrown hedgerows, the County Down main line as it is today. Only the occasional station house or crossing keeper's cottage has survived. Most buildings, even on the remaining line to Bangor, have been demolished. Goods yards have become housing estates or convenient campuses for schools. Here, a widened trunk road has incorporated the railway right-of-way; there, a diverted road made to bridge the line has resumed its old course. But mid-Down has remained a rural backwater and in many places declined in importance as, one by one, the

linen mills closed, while modern farming that needs fewer employees has begun to empty the countryside. Only in north Down has the pace quickened, the place is a virtual suburb of Belfast and the dormitory towns have outgrown their centres, an encouragement to the ring roads and the out-of-town supermarkets.

During these years the Bangor line has proved its usefulness, surviving periods of shabby treatment from the authorities. It was in 1965 that the widening of Middlepath Street leading from the new Queen Elizabeth II Bridge severed the Belfast Central line and reduced the Bangor branch to an isolated rump like the Waterford and Tramore line on the south coast had been throughout its existence.

The Central Railway was to become a ring road; published plans of the time gave the impression that downtown Belfast had a noose around its throat. By this time, flaws in the Ulster Transport Authority had become all too evident; road and rail (finally as we thought) being separated from their fatal embrace in 1968, when Northern Ireland Railways took over what was left of the provincial network. Despite the unsettled conditions of the 1970s the old Central line was rehabilitated and a central station opened in 1976, more or less on the site suggested by the Ulster Railway (and rejected by the BCDR) in 1858. A through service between Bangor and Portadown was successfully established and a new station, Botanic, on the Central line, proved extremely popular.

Though the psychological barrier presented by the *River Lagan* had been surmounted, Central Station is no nearer the city centre than Queen's Quay had been. The concourse at street level has been revamped more than once, but the four sharply curved platform roads represent the limit of what could be done for the accommodation of trains after several acres of railway land had been redistributed between the Housing Executive and that cultural icon of the 1970s, a leisure centre. As Doctor Johnson said, when confronted by the dog that walked on its hind legs . . 'it is remarkable, not that it is done well, but that it is done at all'.

It was confidently expected that a connecting line along the river bank would follow suit to give trains from the former NCC lines access to Central Station. Plans were drawn up and would have gone out to tender, but everything was shelved when Mrs Thatcher's government came to power in 1979. Surprisingly, it was a reactivation of motorway plans in the early 1990s that allowed what came to be known as the 'cross-harbour line' to be built, in parallel with a plan to reopen the former GNR terminus at Great Victoria Street. The inherent meanness of authority has permitted only a single-track viaduct to carry the new link across the *Lagan* beside the multi-lane splendour of the new motorway bridge. The latter wiped out the last traces of Queen's Quay yard, including the old BCDR workshops which had been retained as NIR's Central Service Depot until new premises were built on the site of York Road terminus. The new viaduct has been named the Dargan Bridge to commemorate the celebrated public works contractor who not only reclaimed the sloblands and created the Queen's Island, but was also the long-suffering contractor for the Holywood and Newtownards sections of the BCDR.

Since 1950, with the traffic problems of Belfast worsening annually, the County Down roadbed from Ballymacarrett Junction to Comber has remained largely intact. From time to time, calls are made for its re-use, and one such feasibility study has been announced as these lines are written. It would be a relatively simple exercise to reconnect the Comber line with the present network. However, in a paper, 'Developments on Northern Ireland's Railways', presented to the Irish Railway Record Society and reproduced in its Journal of October 1992, Denis Grimshaw, then General Manager (Projects & Safety) of NIR, gave some interesting examples of current professional thinking. Referring to proposals for electric 'light rail' transport in the Belfast area (not within the NIR remit) he outlined the possibility of the BCDR roadbed to Comber being adopted for this mode, combined with a branch from Dundonald to Newtownards which might use a central reservation on the dual carriageway from Quarry Corner to Newtownards; an appealing concept that would lay the ghost of the original and mistaken route via Comber. One can see that the use of light rail for east Belfast would avoid the overloading of Central Station, a distinct possibility if Ballymacarrett Junction was reinstated. Light rail might well use the old formation right up to an interchange point alongside the present Bridge End halt, and then descend to street level to bring passengers into central Belfast.

Unfortunately for the believer in rail transport (a proven mass people-mover), the recent suggestion of a (guided?) busway on the old alignment may mean the easy option of tarmacadam being adopted.

As for the future of 'heavy rail', the DART electrification which transformed Dublin suburban transport in 1984, caused a few ripples at the other end of the old GNR main line. Electrified services radiating to Bangor, Portadown and Whitehead would be an ideal way to usher Ulster's surviving railway into the new millenium..

Furthermore, with the continuing growth of population in north Down, the time is ripe to rectify the great omission, the lack of a railway between Bangor and Donaghadee.

In the 1950s, the author looked at the map and marvelled at how closely the Bangor and Donaghadee lines approached each other. One envisaged a line diverging at Bangor West and joining the old Donaghadee branch near Ballygrainey – a mere two-and-a-half miles of new railway. It remained a physical possibility for many years, but the spread of housing to the south and west of Bangor since the 1970s has engulfed most of the open country.

Moreover, it is doubtful whether Bangorians would have taken to being left on a stub of railway. One's favourite option now is to extend from Bangor station on a viaduct behind the shops of Main Street and across the former harbour (with a halt to serve the new Marina?) striking east to Ballyholme and running along the seashore towards Glenganagh. This was good enough for Dawlish in Devon and should add a *soupçon* of interest to an otherwise dull promenade. Our line would turn inland there and run more or less parallel to the A2 coast road to Groomsport, approaching Donaghadee behind the Warren. This was the preferred course of entry for other twentieth century schemes, but one cannot imagine any obligation to reinstate the old terminus at the Parade.

Following publication in October 1995 of Government thinking on public transport in the Province (it firmly discounted any use of rail for freight traffic), the appointment of a managing director responsible for all three divisions, NIR, Ulsterbus and Citybus, was announced. There was a change of corporate identity to the overall title 'Translink'. Road-rail co-ordination, which may be interpreted in various ways, had returned. The 28 years of relative freedom for NIR were at an end. Let us hope that all the lessons of the past have been learned.

Acknowledgements and Thanks

In the following pages you will see trains in the Gullet, other trains passing neat farmsteads, running between trim hedgerows and beside summer hayfields, bursting from beneath rugged stone bridges. It is a truism that one picture is worth a thousand words, and having attempted a brief word-picture of the milestones along a century of independent history, let us turn to survey the train in the County Down landscape, thankfully immortalised for us by the camera of William Robb MBE, who, more than any other photographer whose work is presented in this book, has succeeded in capturing the *genius loci* of the Belfast & County Down Railway.

William Robb, doyen of BCDR enthusiasts, is one of the surviving founder-members of the Belfast branch of the Irish Railway Record Society. Most of us had a soft spot for the 'County Down' but being on Belfast's doorstep, its seemed almost too commonplace to photograph.

Through the generosity of Mr Bill Scott it has been possible to include some of the work of that late, great railway eccentric, Drew Donaldson. Drew began to photograph the BCDR just before the Second World War, but few of his early pictures are now in a fit state to reproduce.

The keenest observer of the County Down scene in those days was probably R M Arnold, who did not suffer fools gladly. 'Mac' was not a photographer but towards the end of his life put his impressions into print, and his book *The County Down* (Irish Steam Scene, 1981) is worthy of examination for his studies of railway personalities.

Reg Ludgate, who was a great recorder of Belfast tramways (much to Drew Donaldson's disgust!) shared many railway jaunts with the author when film and cash were scarce and the only equipment available was the humble box camera.

The greatest help and encouragement to the present writer came from John Harold Houston, one-time Works Manager at York Road LMS (NCC), who occupied a similar position at Queen's Quay workshops under the UTA until their sudden closure in 1950. Harold was one of those rare beings, both professional railwayman and a railway historian. He was an absolute fount of information, readily imparted to those who asked.

Unstinting help in locomotive matters came also from another great railway historian, Bob Clements. It is sad to reflect on the passing of so many knowledgeable friends whose constructive criticism would have been welcome at this time.

Thanks are due also to the following: Dr Donald B McNeill, Messrs Chris Aspinwall, Gerry Cochrane of the Downpatrick Steam Railway, Joe Lloyd, Clifton Flewitt, Herbert Richards, Dick Riley, Peter Rowledge and Cecil Slator. Richard Casserley's patient help in supplying prints from his father's negatives is much appreciated; Henry Casserley's presence at Queen's Quay in the 1930s enabled him to record the engines in the more elaborate livery that disappeared under the grime of the Second World War.

Pictures from the E S Russell Collection that evoke the spirit of the County Down in its last days are reproduced by the kindness of Mr Clive Taylor and that superb photographer Mr John Dewing has come up trumps with locomotive studies of 1946, a rather rare vintage.

In attempting maximum coverage of the system half a century after closure, one realizes that few of us in those days had begun to appreciate that there was more to be recorded than locomotives and trains, nor did we know that the extinction of the BCDR would be so complete and so rapid. However, the gaps in this coverage would be greater if the yardstick of perfection was applied throughout. Certain aspects of the BCDR never appear to have been photographed, even 'modern' installations like the Drumhirk ballast quarry whose siding lasted until 1942. For most of the Company's history there had been a rather variable traffic in stone from the quarries at Scrabo and Ballygowan. The 'stone train' was a regular feature in the working timetable; most stone was carried in owners' wagons – quite an unusual sight on Irish metals. All these were everyday activities and taken for granted by the local population. Perhaps we should count ourselves lucky to have salvaged as much of the past as we have, and why, in one or two instances, where no alternative could be found, pictures have had to be used whose quality has left something to be desired,

All photographs not credited to others were taken by the author.

QUEEN'S QUAY
AND THE HARBOUR LINES

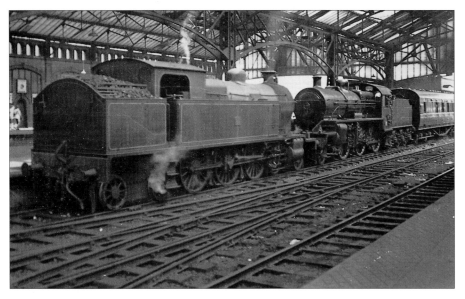

Above: **This 1949 interior view of the 1912 train shed gives some idea of its solid construction, although it was soon to be stripped of its roof glazing. NCC Mogul No 94 *The Maine*, is the cuckoo in the nest here, for she melted a lead plug when running-in on the Bangor line on 13th May 1949 and was towed back to Belfast in triumph by BCDR Baltic tank No 23 – her crew grinning from ear to ear.**

Below: **The UTA's first diesel multiple unit, AEC-engined cars Nos 6 and 7, with a trailer coach in the middle, is incidental to this interior view of Queen's Quay train shed on 22nd August 1951, included to show more of the robust structural steelwork. The patent glazing has already been removed, and there are winters of discontent in store for passengers until the umbrella roofing over platforms 3 and 4 is extended as far as the main concourse.**

QUEEN'S QUAY

The Belfast terminus which was opened to Holywood traffic on 2nd August 1848 was a temporary building a little to the north of the permanent structure, which was then under construction. Vacated by Holywood trains when they were admitted to the latter on 19th December 1850, the wooden train shed became the first BCDR repair shop and was in that part of the terminus handed over to the Belfast, Holywood & Bangor Railway in 1865.

Scrabo Street on the south side of the terminus gave access to the original goods yard and took its name from the hill outside Newtownards where a particularly attractive vein of building stone was quarried, and unloaded at the 'Stone Bank' in the yard. The adjacent goods shed of 1850 became successively a carriage and wagon shop and a centrally heated carriage shed known as the Vinery from its subtropical warmth.

A permanent locomotive shed and workshops were built in the late 1850s, their architect being one de Witt Gray, whose commission also included station buildings and facilities from Comber to Ballynahinch and Downpatrick.

The nucleus of the BHBR station was an additional island platform with glazed iron canopy built alongside the main train shed and first used in March 1860. It vanished in the 1884 reconstruction.

The BCDR 'Old Yard' was inadequate for traffic by 1867, when a new goods yard was laid out to the north of the BHBR station. An iron framed goods store for this yard was usefully dismantled and redistributed among the departments on construction of the 1893 warehouse, a very imposing building for a railway whose goods revenue was only a fraction of passenger receipts. Even so, a second goods store was needed by 1911.

The new terminus of this period has been discussed briefly in the Introduction; now let the photographs speak for themselves.

Above: **The Saturdays-only 'Golfers Express' for Newcastle at platform 2 on 2nd July 1949 is headed by a famous survivor. After its wartime rebuild, 2-4-0 No 6 had gravitated to lesser duties once more. Surprisingly, the UTA retubed her and she was a regular feature of the main line to the very last. One suspects that the motivation came from that great enthusiast, Harold Houston.**

Below: **Between main line duties, 2-4-2T No 27 shunts empty carriages at platform 2 on 19th September 1949. Normally used on the Ardglass branch, she made the return trip to Belfast in that last summer of the** County Down. The 6-compartment third on the right of picture stands on the so-called 'North Siding'; its name reminds us that platforms 4 and 5 occupied the site of the former BHBR terminus.

Above right: **Rare in the British Isles, though not unique, were the tram sidings of Belfast Corporation Transport that served both Queen's Quay and York Road Stations. An efficient service was maintained between the city centre and both stations, as well as the GNR terminus, where trams passed the entrance. Printed timetables were exhibited at the stations, trams being timed to make connections** with train arrivals and departures. This is the tram bay at Queen's Quay, which could hold two cars. The Scrabo Street pedestrian entrance is alongside and the concourse can be seen in the background. The inevitable phasing-out of the tramways took place in the early 1950s. This late photograph taken on 21st April 1953 shows 'Chamberlain' car No 357 on a working between Queen's Quay and the Shankill Road. This was the last tramway link with the city centre. No 357 was preserved and is now in the Ulster Folk and Transport Museum at Cultra.

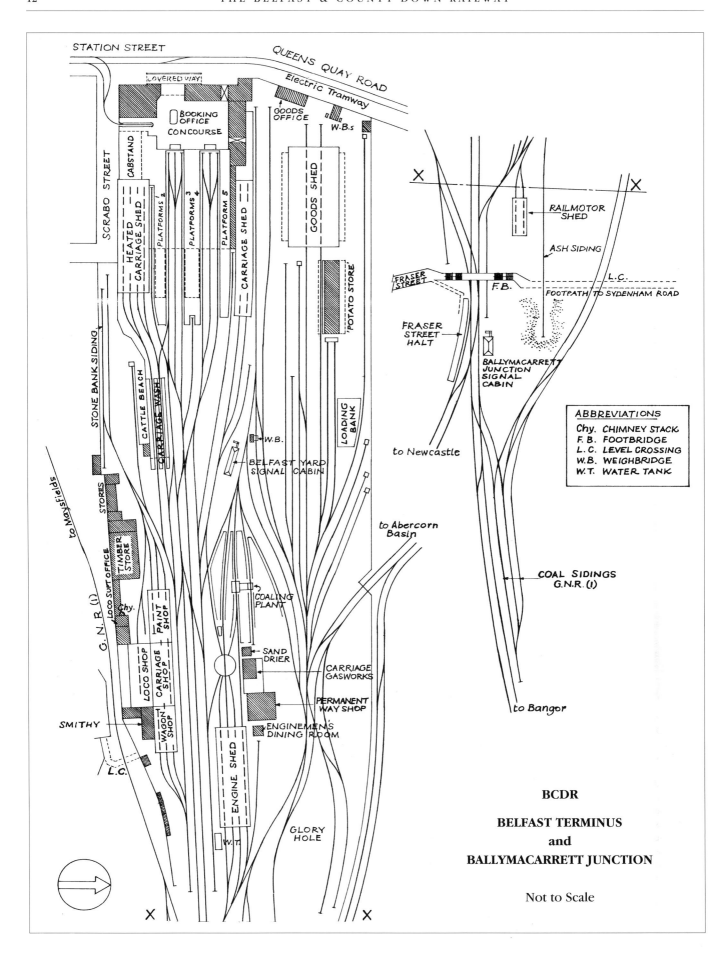

STATION STREET

QUEENS QUAY ROAD

Electric Tramway

COVERED WAY

BOOKING OFFICE
CONCOURSE

GOODS OFFICE

W.B.s

SCRABO STREET

CABSTAND

HEATED CARRIAGE SHED

PLATFORMS 1

PLATFORMS 3

PLATFORM 5

CARRIAGE SHED

GOODS SHED

POTATO STORE

RAILMOTOR SHED

ASH SIDING

FRASER STREET

F.B.

L.C.

FOOTPATH TO SYDENHAM ROAD

FRASER STREET HALT

BALLYMACARRETT JUNCTION SIGNAL CABIN

STONE BANK SIDING

CATTLE BEACH

CARRIAGE WASH

W.B.

BELFAST YARD SIGNAL CABIN

LOADING BANK

to Newcastle

to Maysfields

STORES

LOCO SUPT OFFICE

TIMBER STORE

G.N.R. (I)

Chy.

PAINT SHOP

LOCO SHOP

CARRIAGE SHOP

WAGON SHOP

SMITHY

L.C.

ENGINE SHED

COALING PLANT

SAND DRIER

CARRIAGE GASWORKS

PERMANENT WAY SHOP

ENGINEMEN'S DINING ROOM

GLORY HOLE

W.T.

to Abercorn Basin

COAL SIDINGS G.N.R. (I)

to Bangor

ABBREVIATIONS
Chy. CHIMNEY STACK
F. B. FOOTBRIDGE
L. C. LEVEL CROSSING
W.B. WEIGHBRIDGE
W.T. WATER TANK

BCDR

BELFAST TERMINUS
and
BALLYMACARRETT JUNCTION

Not to Scale

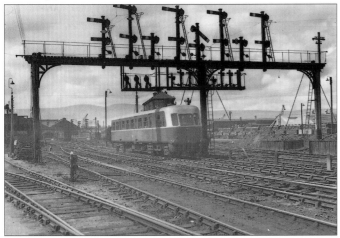

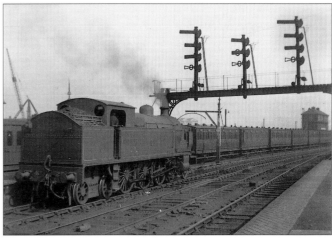

Top: **The salient features of this view are pure BCDR, however things are not quite the same . . . the Company's newest locomotive has been renumbered 209, but what is it doing on the 1.20pm to Holywood? It is March 1950, the 2-4-2 tanks have all gone, and there is spare motive power. The erstwhile push-and-pull set still uses the former control trailer as a brake-open third and superior classes have their less-comfortable 6-wheeled composite, but the leading coach is a brake-third the wrong way round. The magnificent gantry (the Bridge of Signals in official parlance) is mostly obscured by 209's crisp exhaust. There is plenty of locomotive coal in the stacks to the right.**

Above left: **Sentinel-Ganz railcar No 5 had run trials in England before the Second World War and, re-gauged to 5ft 3in, was the first item of diesel motive power acquired by the UTA. It was a very unwise purchase that is not part of this story, but the view taken on 27th April 1951 gives a complete picture of the Bridge of Signals. Home signals and calling-on arms for each of the platform roads can be clearly identified, signals between them controlling access to the two run-round roads and the North Siding; the latter uses the same post as the up advanced starter. The lower deck of shunting dolls seems to cover every possible permutation of the yard layout. To the right of the picture it**

may be observed that in the former goods yard, BCDR 6-wheelers are being assembled for auction as scrap.

Above right: **No 25 takes water at the platform end on 24th March 1949. Beyond, the 'Holywood Yard' sidings, another throw-back to BHBR days, are full of stock awaiting the evening rush. The gantries that figure so prominently in pictures of Queen's Quay had their signal lamps lit by oil-gas which was piped into the station. After the Second World War the Company took the bold step of substituting electric lighting for gas on these gantries.**

Above: **Queen's Quay yard, looking towards Ballymacarrett Junction, on 12th May 1950, with coal stacks, sand drier, gasworks and the Permanent Way shop on the left, along with part of the west front of the running shed. Fraser Street footbridge is in the distance and, right, the carriage and wagon shops. The taller portion of building alongside the south headshunt had been the first engine shed. The unconventional railcar making for platform 2 is LMS (NCC) No 2, sent over to handle the Holywood short workings.**

Centre left: **Large 4-4-2T No 208 passes the running shed on an off-peak Bangor train of four NCC bogies, half the full rake transferred in 1948 and still working the peak-hour expresses. The rather stunted outer home signal against the east gable of the wagon shop had to be visible underneath Fraser Street footbridge.**

Left: **On 27th June 1950 former LMS(NCC) U2 class 4-4-0 No 79 *Kenbaan Castle* has arrived for overhaul at the old BCDR shops and is seen at the coal stacks having its tender emptied and smokebox cleaned. The coaling plant in the background was built shortly after the Second World War, when a new Taylor & Hubbard diesel crane, numbered C2, was also supplied to assist in coal and ash handling. Its steam-powered predecessor went to the East Downshire quay at Dundrum. To our disappointment, Queen's Quay works were closed quite suddenly and No 79 was sent back to York Road for completion of its heavy overhaul and, consequently it was not 'run-in' on the Bangor line.**

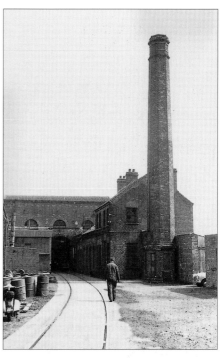

Above left: **The west elevation of the carriage paint shop in April 1967, which by now a railcar servicing depot. The building behind the smokestack had been the Locomotive Superintendent's office.**

Above right: **The right-hand track on the previous picture leads into the former loco-motive shops. The 'saw-tooth' roof, common to carriage and loco shops, has been altered by the UTA to arc-section roofing, seen here.**

Below: **No 217 was the only 'bogie tank' to be given the UTA lined black livery. Here, it is shunting wagons in the goods yard on 10th May 1950.**

Above: **A Bangor train leaves behind No 24 on 6th June 1949. It is formed by a 'half set' including one of the 1938 tri-composites. The leading coach is a 5-compartment first, exclusive to the Bangor line.**

No 7 is on empty coaching stock duties in the Old Yard to the left. E S Russell

Below: **No 6 shunts empty stock in the passenger yard on 6th June 1949.**
E S Russell

Above: **No 13 bustles in with a Donaghadee train on the same date. A big 4-4-2T is on the turntable and two other engines are glimpsed outside the running shed.**
E S Russell

Below: **On 28th March 1948, No 23 passes the running shed with an up Bangor train. Many shed windows were bricked up for ARP (Air Raid Precautions) reasons during the Second World War, and along with** economies like the removal of roof ventilators this did nothing for the shed's appearance. The three turnouts from the headshunt in foreground lead into the wagon shop. E S Russell

Above: **Muscle-power turns the versatile No 26 on the Queen's Quay table, in 1949. Also in the picture are gas storage cylinders where the two gasholder trucks were charged. On the right, wagons are under repair outside the shops. Industrial Ballymacarrett is in the background.** Joe Lloyd

Centre: **At least hundreds of solo engine pictures were taken outside Queen's Quay sheds down the years, but general views of the yard seem rare. In this view taken on 13th October 1950, the locomotives from left to right are Nos 218, 220, 211, 4, 223.**

Bottom: **The scene at the end of the same month, where No 220 had derailed on the turntable during the previous evening. The Adelaide breakdown crane from the GNR is lowering driving and trailing wheels back on to the rails. The engine had not fallen right into the pit, but never ran again. She was said to have suffered a cracked frame; perhaps the fall opened an old wound.**

Photograph on the opposite page:

Bottom: **Seen in March 1946, heading a train of BCDR open wagons on the Sydenham Road, No 29 has been repainted in the dark olive green, which was first introduced in 1937. This locomotive was later renumbered 229 by the UTA.**

THE BELFAST HARBOUR LINES

Wharves along Queen's Quay and around the later Abercorn Basin were largely given over to the import of coal. The quayside was first served by rail in 1852 when a siding from the BCDR terminus was laid across Station Street to a wagon turntable providing access to a line along the quay. The Belfast Harbour Commissioners built the Abercorn Basin in 1867, served by a tramway from the BCDR goods yard that emerged through gates in the company's north boundary.

The Harbour Commissioners purchased the old quay siding from the BCDR and extended it to join their new tramway system. It should perhaps be emphasised that the 'Harbour Tramways' were 5ft 3ins gauge and laid in grooved rail that accepted wheels of standard railway profile. Arrival of the Central Railway at Ballymacarrett, and at Donegall Quay before that, provided the incentive for the Commissioners to lay tramways along all quaysides as the port expanded. Growth of the shipyards on Queen's Island brought further complexity, and on electrification of the Belfast street tramways the Station Street line (originally built but not operated by the BCDR) was in 1908 extended along Queens Road to serve the yards of Harland & Wolff and Workman Clarke.

This 4ft 9ins tramway ran parallel to a single track 5ft 3ins line that threw off sundry branches, crossing the electric tramway, to reach into cavernous engineering shops. All this trackage was paved in square-setts. At the Abercorn Basin, the Corporation trams had to contend with a right angled crossing of three parallel railway tracks leading to the BCDR goods yard and the GNR coal sidings at Ballymacarrett.

A further Harbour Commissioners' line ran eastwards along Sydenham Road to oil storage depots.

The BCDR shunting engine No 29 and the Great Northern 0-6-4Ts that inspired its design were constantly at work on these harbour tramways.

Above: **On 6th May 1953 No 214 is seen propelling empty wagons towards the quayside. She was deputizing for 0-6-4T No 229 when the latter was being overhauled in York Road shops, and later replaced No 229 altogether on this duty, a task for which she was quite unsuited.**

The last home-based BCDR engine to be steamed, No 214 was cut up in full view of the passenger station; it was like watching an autopsy on an old friend. On the skyline rise the tower-cranes of what was once the largest ship building complex in the world. The huge slipway gantries on the left were

the nightly roost of thousands of starlings whose sunset aerobatics in enormous formations were quite spectacular. The waiting tram is one of the 'McCreary' streamliners of 1935, the class names were those of the General Managers who introduced each type.

Above: **When No 229 was being overhauled in June 1950, one of the two Fowler tanks built by the LMS and re-gauged for the NCC during the Second World War, was sent from York Road as a substitute. Here No 18 waits for her next spell of duty close by the gate that gave access from Queen's Quay yard to the Harbour lines.**

Below: **No 14, by now 214, the last BCDR tender engine still working, seen on the Abercorn Basin tramway crossing. She is running tender-first towards Queen's Quay yard. Note the flagman who had to precede all locomotive workings on the Harbour Commissioners' tramways. No 214 retained the 'invisible green' livery to the end, and**

close up, the BCDR's coat-of-arms could just be made out under the grime on cab and tender sides. The date is 6th May 1953.

THE LINE TO DONAGHADEE

BALLYMACARRETT JUNCTION

Brought into full use as an interchange point with the Belfast Central Railway on 12th May 1876, the complexities of this railway crossroads – where there were originally five double junctions in the layout – were simplified in later years. When the junction was abolished in 1965 it consisted of two sets of facing points, with an intermediate trailing crossover on the double-track Bangor line, all that remained of the BCDR, to say nothing of the Belfast Central. Fraser Street footbridge across the two railways was provided by Belfast Corporation to alleviate the constant trespass by shipyard workers resident in the locality. It gave its name to Fraser Street Halt, a timber platform erected alongside the up line almost at the junction itself in 1928. This gave 'Islandmen' commuting from the main line a similar facility to Ballymacarrett Halt on the Bangor line. The junction layout precluded provision of a down platform for those homeward bound, who had to use Queen's Quay.

Right: **The depressing surroundings of Fraser Street Halt are all too evident in this easterly prospect of Ballymacarrett Junction. The Central line comes in on the right and the BCDR main line begins its 1 in 124 climb almost immediately. Out of sight to the left of the Bangor line, the GNR coal sidings diverge. The up junction signals on both main and branch lines were similar, each carried a distant for the Home Cabin and a skeleton arm on the main post guarding a facing crossover admitting trains to Queen's Quay goods yard. The date is 26th March 1946, and a GNR railcar, borrowed from the Dublin suburban services, is working off-peak trains on the Bangor line. This was the time of Great Northern management of the BCDR.**

Below: **Great Northern 0-6-4T No 22 comes off the Central line with empty oil tanks bound for the Sydenham Road depots. The BCDR down junction signals are immediately right of the locomotive. Also in the picture is the four arm junction** signal for movements from Queen's Quay goods yard. The arms, top to bottom, are for the GNR coal sidings, down Bangor line, down main line and up main line. The date is 31st January 1950.

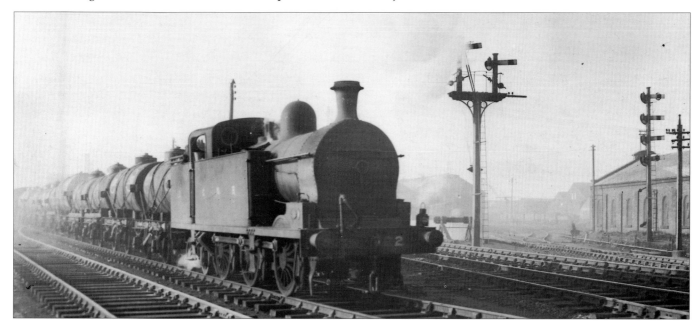

Above: **Taken from Fraser Street platform on 31st January 1950, wintry sunshine lights 4-4-2T No 13 as it heads the 1.10pm train to Donaghadee through the Junction. The 'Dee' train had a bogie brake-third as well as the bogie lavatory-composite, with an ancient 6-wheel passenger brake at the rear. Ballymacarrett Junction and Queen's Quay Home cabins were contemporaneous. The Ballymacarrett nameboard has scarlet edging and letters against a light stone background.**

Centre left: **Belatedly, Comber commuters are offered the comfort of a half set of modern NCC stock. The 12.50pm working to Comber on 27th March 1950 passes under Fraser Street footbridge behind No 203, which is about to take the former BCDR main line at Ballymacarrett Junction.**

Left: **A general view east from Fraser Street platform on 10th May 1950. Part of the double junction leading to the GNR sidings can be seen to the right of NCC railcar No 2. The main line has closed by this time, but remains intact.**

Above: **Freight movements on the Central line had increased since closure of the BCDR goods depot at Queen's Quay. No 29 is on GNR metals as she approaches Ballymacarrett Junction with a cattle train in 1949. The BCDR railmotor shed is in the background, across the tracks behind the crumbling boundary wall.** Joe Lloyd

Centre right: **A good rear view of the down junction signals on 1st March 1950 as WT class No 53 approaches with old BCDR stock on the 1.17pm Bangor train. To the left of the picture, the Belfast Central line, singled in 1928, comes in from behind the BCDR workshops.**

Right: **An afternoon Newtownards goods climbs Club Row bank out of Bally-macarrett on 20th April 1950, two days before the Donaghadee line was closed. A 4-4-2 tank engine seems a surprising choice for a train of this length, but No 211 was coping very well on the incline. By this time the big 0-6-0 No 4 was on the NCC section while her sisters Nos 10 and 26 had not run since the main line closed, leaving only No 14 among the 0-6-0s, which was obviously unavailable for this goods working.**

BLOOMFIELD

Opened in May 1879, construction of the Bloomfield station was sponsored by a firm of local speculative builders, Sinclair & Boyd.

Free season tickets were issued to house purchasers for a given period by the BCDR. Berkeley Wise designed the two-storey brick station building, situated on the Belfast side of Beersbridge Road level crossing. Wise was later responsible for the engineering work when the line to Knock was doubled and the up platform with waiting shed was provided.

A lattice footbridge was built alongside the level crossing, immediately beyond was the signal cabin and trailing crossover. The latter was installed in connection with a short siding that trailed into the up line, serving a stone depot owned by one of the Ballygowan quarry-masters. It was in use from 1893 to 1926.

Left: **The unusual rostering of 2-4-2T No 27 on the 2.20pm down Newcastle added spice to the last summer of main line operation. On 30th June 1949, No 27 makes plenty of smoke approaching Bloomfield. Comber will be her first stop. The train formation was unorthodox too, the leading vehicle is 6-wheel brake-third, No 51, built in 1888 and not long out of the shops in full BCDR livery. Both No 51 and the following bogie brake-third have their guards' compartments at the rear. Punctilious BCDR train marshalling was on the way out.**

Below: **No 15 arrives at Bloomfield with the 1.10pm train to Donaghadee on 6th April 1949. Berkeley Wise's handsome station is seen in part behind the footbridge. This engineer had little chance to leave his mark on BCDR architecture, most of his time was spent improving the deplorable permanent way he had inherited.**

KNOCK

Trains began calling at 'the crossing at Bally-cloughan Nursery', (Knock Road) from 30th December 1850.

The station was on the down side of the crossing and a hut, part of the temporary station at Holywood, became the Knock booking office. It was replaced by a brick station building in 1869. Knock had for many years been the terminus for 'short trains' from Belfast, the operation of which was conducted in a highly irregular fashion.

On the doubling of the line the station became a block post, with a crossover at both ends after the double road had been continued to Comber in 1893. There was a lattice footbridge at the crossing and the signal cabin was on the new up platform.

Above: **There are occasions when the appearance of a train in a station photograph, however appealing, conceals important features that might be lost for ever. On 20th July 1933 the photographer has Knock station to himself, capturing lattice footbridge, crossing gates and station house in a nice composition. The booking office is at rail level and Culverwell has provided his lineside paling along the ramp to discourage dangerous short cuts across the line. The station nameboard is in its pre-war colours of white or cream lettering and border on a maroon background. Among the better-known Bovril and Virol enamelled advertisements is one for Sawers, the Belfast fishmongers – it depicts an unlucky salmon on the hook, being drawn out of the water.** W Robb

Right: **There is something almost Arcadian about this view of Knock on 4th July 1933. As No 20 enters with the 1.11pm train to Comber, the cheerful profusion of the Stationmaster's garden is noteworthy, as is the 'up wrong line starter', cantilevered from the station house wall. One would like to know the stresses involved when this signal was pulled off, and whether the wall of the 1869 building had to be reinforced.** W Robb

Above: **High summer at Dundonald. It is 5th July 1933, and the presence of that great all-rounder No 26 on the 12.50pm Comber train is a measure of the extra traffic being handled that day. The station building is on the left and Culverwell's standard waiting shed can be partly seen on the opposite platform, behind the train.** W.Robb

Left: **De Witt Gray's Comber station frontage a few years after services had ceased. Like his other station buildings, it is built of local whinstone – probably obtained from 'The Gullet' – and replete with brick quoins and arches. A Culverwell porch was rather out of place, but is seen to be disintegrating.**

DUNDONALD

COMBER

One of the original main line stations, Dundonald remained a ramshackle wooden affair until rebuilt in 1900, when a separate Stationmaster's house was added. Before that, the doubling of the line to Comber had necessitated a new down platform and waiting shed, in 1893, when Dundonald also became a block post with crossovers permitting reversal of local trains when required. The sparse goods traffic was handled at the platforms until a siding was put down on the up side in 1901. Dundonald cabin was on the up platform; its abolition was proposed in 1926 when signals were altered and a crossover was removed, but every summer until closure the cabin continued to be switched in.

For the uninitiated, Comber is pronounced as in cucumber. Nevertheless, locals call it 'Cummer' and they are right, for in old Gaelic it is An Comar, still surviving in the name of a mythical inhabitant, 'Cummer Ann'. It may also be cognate with the Welsh *cymer,* a small valley.

The Comber station of 1850 was a timber-built structure with one platform on the northeast or 'town' side of the single line. A siding and cattle platform had been provided by the following year, while a substantial goods store in masonry was built in 1852 for the sum of £490. What seems to have been the same store remained in use up to closure, and still exists as a council depot. A bypass road has obliterated all other traces of Comber station.

The junction station of 1858 had two long platforms connected by a subway, station buildings and goods store being on the up side. There was a third track between the platform roads, the layout arranged 'to suit the arrival and departure of three trains at the same moment'. So said the Board minutes, but readers are invited to guess the logistics involved. The Andrews family, strong supporters of the BCDR through the years, built a large flax-spinning mill in the fork between the Donaghadee and Downpatrick lines. For this a siding was laid in during 1863 and building materials for the factory came by rail. Messrs Andrews continued to send their products and receive their coal through the siding right up to closure.

Right: **An overall view of the layout at Comber, looking in the down direction, taken on 20th April 1950.**

Centre right: **It is 20th August 1932, the day of the Tourist Trophy races, and No 19 stands at the head of the 'shuttle' that takes racegoers to the grandstand at Comber No 2 level crossing, known locally as Glass Moss. Coupled to the last carriage is 0-6-0 No 4 which will lead on the return journey. Wooden platforms were erected on either side of the crossing (they accommodated only five of the coaches) and a temporary footbridge allowed spectators and through passengers to cross the road between platforms. The eight-coach train appears to consist in its entirety of vintage Oldbury 6-wheelers, making it third class only.**
W Robb

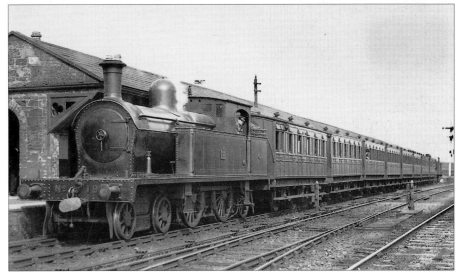

Below: **On Easter Monday, 11th April 1939, No 18 pilots No 30 on the 4.45pm down train to Newcastle. Piloting was uncommon on the BCDR, and one engine may have had other duties ahead. The first class saloon is No 53, the 1889 'State Carriage'; next to it is a 4-compartment Ashbury first of 1891.** W Robb

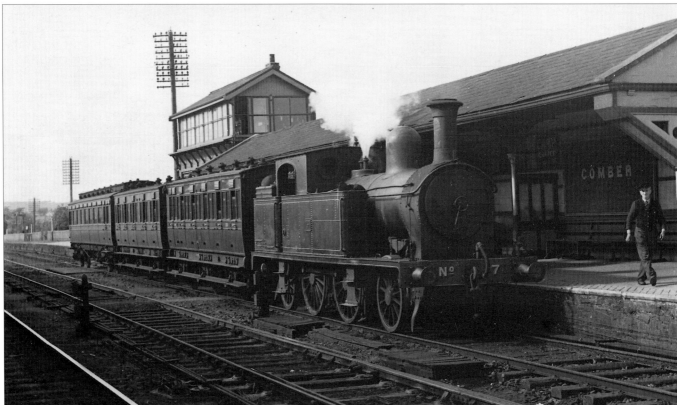

Top: **On 6th June 1949, No 15 enters on a 10-coach Donaghadee train. The first coach is a standard 6-compartment Second, followed by no less than six of the Oldbury veterans, suggesting an excursion working.** E S Russell

Above: **On the same day, 6th June 1949, a 'Holywood Motor' set arrives on a short working from Belfast. No 7 had been repainted in full BCDR livery under UTA auspices, and earned a mild reproof for Harold Houston, who shouldn't have ordered a repaint for such an elderly** specimen. **The rest of us were very pleased with it, however! On the abolition of push-pull working, a 6-wheel brake-third was added to one end of the auto set. This example is a 5-compartment Ashbury built carriage of 1893. The middle coach is a first-second composite.** E S Russell

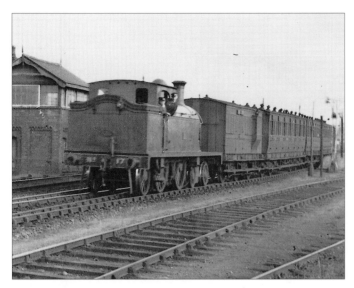

Above: **No 17 and the 6.05pm up 'Dee' train are passing the old North signal cabin at Comber in August 1939. Part of Comber goods yard is in the foreground.** W Robb

Above right: **A major resignalling exercise was carried out in 1925. A new Central** cabin was built on the down platform and the North and South cabins, dating from the remodelling of the 1890s, were closed. Here is the Central cabin on 4th May 1932, exhibiting posters of the 1930s for Bushmills Whiskey, Cadbury's Chocolate and Keating's Insect Powder. They sum up the state of the nation. W Robb

Below: **Evening sunshine on 15th July 1933 brings detail into sharp relief on No 13 and her train. The 6.18pm to Donaghadee has the road, but somebody is in earnest conversation with the crew, and an off-side guard's door has swung open.** W Robb

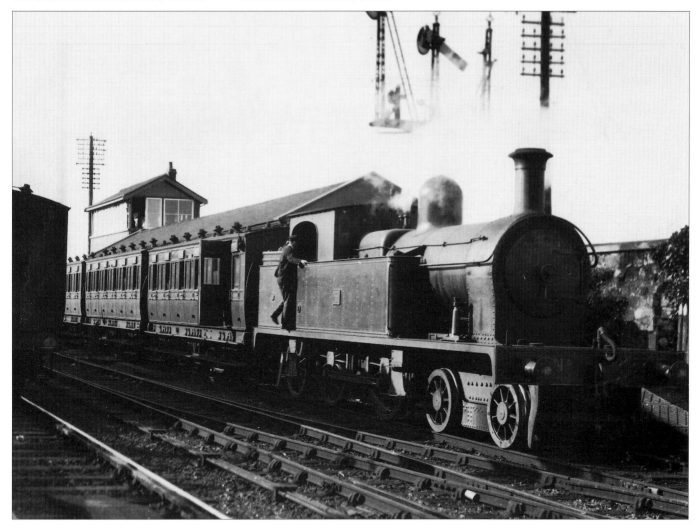

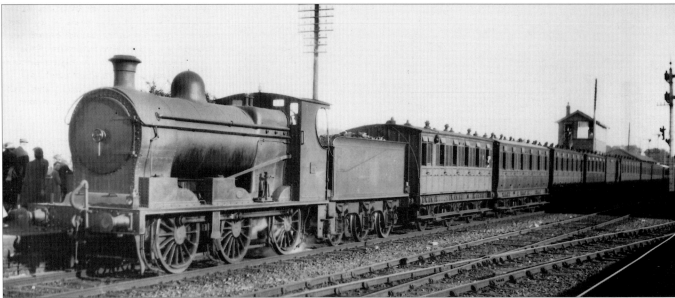

Top: **The 'bogie tanks' looked nice in pairs. On 22nd July 1949 this pairing was a matter of operating convenience. No 30 had come down with the 12.50pm from Belfast. No 15 had brought in the 12.35pm from Ballynahinch and handed it over to diesel No 2, that was just out of the shops. No 2 left with the Ballynahinch train, and the pair of tanks shunted the 12.50 rake to the up platform and would take it to Belfast as the 1.40pm train.**

Above, centre: **No 10 leaves Comber on a nicely assorted train carrying homeward bound racegoers on 7th September 1935. The semaphore signal with subsidiary arms on the right of the picture was used by trains running through on the middle road. It was removed by the UTA in 1949. W Robb**

Left: **Comber Junction on 22nd July 1949 as No 13 pulls out with the 1.30pm Belfast to Donaghadee working. One of the automatic tablet catchers is in the left foreground, covered by a canvas hood.**

Above: **On 19th September 1949, the BCDR atmosphere has not dispersed. No 26 leaves Comber with the Ballynahinch branch set of two 6-wheelers. This extension of the branch service allowed a handy connection in both directions with the Donaghadee line. The Harlandic diesel locomotive No 2, normally used on the branch, must have been indisposed that day.**

Left: **The diesel-electric locomotive No 2 is in good-health this time, on the Comber to Ballynahinch working on 22nd July 1949.**

Below: **Andrews' Siding curves into the mill yard. The siding parallel to the main line has a loop serving the wagon weighbridge. The date is 20th April 1950.**

NEWTOWNARDS

Newtownard's second station, which opened on 3rd June 1861, was a somewhat unpopular replacement for the 1850 terminus, situated as it was on the hillside behind the town. It was awkwardly laid out following a series of mistakes by the resident engineer. Although modernised in 1896 with two platforms and a passing loop, it remained difficult to work. The entrance to the yard was a facing connection on the down loop, that crossed the up line within a short distance of the commodious goods store. The left-hand store road was called the 'table road', in memory of a locomotive turntable sited there in error. Why Newtownards needed a turntable in the 1860s is anyone's guess. In spite of all this, the yard was one of the busiest on the BCDR.

Top: **A down goods enters Newtownards in early 1950. The connection to the goods yard is in the foreground. To shunt the yard, No 211 will have to run round its train and propel wagons into the sidings as required. The subway to the up platform is on right of the signal cabin.** E M Patterson

Centre left: **Newtownards goods yard, seen from the platform end in the previous picture. There is a generous goods store, but shunting the yard meant constant occupation of both up and down loops. The cattle beach is on the left, and on the extreme right is Charles Neill's coal depot. By this time coal was no longer imported through Donaghadee but came by road from Bangor harbour. The coal merchants consequently lost the rent rebate granted by the railway company. There is a rather rare vehicle on the right-hand siding – one of the Great Northern's bogie grain wagons, which would have been based at Queen's bridge goods station in Belfast. One guesses it has brought grain for the maltings on the Greyabbey Road. These wagons were originally built for Guinness traffic. The date is 6th June 1949.**

Left: **On the same day as the previous view, No 15, unusually bunker first, enters with an up passenger train.**

Right: **Having left its train clear of the yard crossing, No 15 runs back along the down loop and into the yard. She picks up the cattle wagon at the beach and returns in the same fashion, to place the wagon at the head of her train.**

Centre right: **The 1861 station building was a 'one off' and built of the pleasant variegated sandstone from Scrabo quarries, on the other side of Newtownards. This view was taken after closure, on 27th May 1956.**

Below: **By an odd coincidence, Eric Russell also visited Newtownards on the same day as the author, 6th June 1949. No 13 enters from Donaghadee, and if the shadows are anything to go by, this was slightly later in the day. Was No 15 on the 3.15pm up and No 13 on the 4.30pm?** E S Russell

BALLYGRAINEY

Situated conveniently near the multiple crossroads known as Six Road Ends, two arms of which extended to Bangor and the fishing village of Groomsport, each about four miles away, Ballygrainey's facilities were minimal: one passenger platform and one goods siding. Yet it was a block post and although the cabin

had been closed before the Second World War it was reopened in 1941 and remained officially in use until the end. It did however spend a lot of time switched out of use. The lever frame and block instruments were housed in a shed on the platform, totally unlike the neat brick signal cabins characteristic of the BCDR.

Bottom left: **Ballygrainey Halt's up starting and down home signals were both on the one post.**

Above: **No 219 passes with an up train from Donaghadee. The signal cabin, the lean-to hut which can be seen at the far end of the platform, is switched out.**

Below right: **Looking towards Donaghadee from the single platform; the Stationmaster's house is on the right.**

All the photographs on this page were taken by the author on 15th April 1950.

DONAGHADEE

While officialdom was making up its mind about the Portpatrick steamer, Donaghadee passenger terminus was a temporary expedient. A couple of houses on the Parade were purchased and a platform and run-round, covered by the old goods shed roof from Newtownards, were built in a back-yard. And so it remained until the end of its railway career and beyond, into UTA omnibus days. The platform was lengthened later, and a bay added. The purpose-built goods store was more orthodox, and an engine shed and turntable were provided at the outer end of the yard. A siding to the pier built in 1870, handled a sizeable coal traffic, a Newtownards firm imported coal using its own steamer. The sharp bend in the pier was no obstacle to coal wagons, but it is difficult to envisage the BCDR carrying out its intention of 'placing carriages alongside the Steamer when put upon the Station'. A later addition to station amenities was the 'Railway Pavilion', a timber building let out to organized excursions, such as Sunday School bunfights.

Top: **From the Parade, Donaghadee terminus was an unhappy-looking station. It had looked rather better when it had been a three-storey building, which included a railway owned hotel, but an infestation of dry-rot between the wars necessitated removal of the top floor and construction of a new roof. Here it is on 6th June 1949; it was not improved in its later life as a bus station.** E S Russell

Centre: **The goods store, water tank, signal cabin and engine shed all feature in this general view of Donaghadee yard, taken on 12th July 1949. The two-road locomotive shed dates from 1922. Its agricultural character hints at stringent economy.**

Bottom: **Seen on the 17th April 1950, the Harbour siding diverged from the bay platform road, and had a loop for the wagon weighbridge.**

Left: **Donaghadee's train shed. with No 15 on the 1.25pm up train, looking from the cattle beach, on 7th June 1937.** W Robb

Below: **No 15, last seen at Newtownards, is taking water at Donaghadee and has been turned, before she couples up to her train. The passenger van and leading four coaches seem to have been the normal complement during that day, 6th June 1949. The string of Oldburys seen on the down working at Comber (see the top picture on page 28) are ready to take their excursionists back to Belfast.** E S Russell

Top right: **The last day of railway services to Donaghadee, 22nd April 1950, was a miserable, wet and melancholy occasion, summed up by this view inside the train shed, showing the roof trusses from the original Newtownards goods store. Two caravan coaches provided by the UTA are stored under cover, for the winter. They re-emerged for the 1950 season and remained in use for several years, standing on a detached portion of track.**

Centre right: **This seaside view provides a glimpse (on the right) of the outer reaches of Donaghadee yard. The double slip point on the headshunt gives access across the goods store siding to the turntable road which at this time is host to the two caravan coaches sent down by the UTA. They are on the approximate site of the previous engine shed. It is 12th July 1949 and No 19 arrives with a train from Belfast.**

Bottom right: **Photographs of goods trains on the Donaghadee line are hard to find. Here, circa 1938, is No 26 leading one out of the goods yard. The train consists of just four goods and cattle wagons and a brake van.** Drew Donaldson

Below: **The station approaches, showing the home signals reading to the main and bay platforms with a shunt-ahead arm for the goods yard. The two-road engine shed is in the distance behind the signal. The Railway Pavilion, signal cabin and water tank are also visible.** H M Rea

THROUGH THE HEART
OF COUNTY DOWN

ROBB COUNTRY

The County Down main line south of Comber skirted the family farm of William Robb. His photographs of the trains in the County Down Landscape form the basis of the first part of this chapter. No other photographer recorded this aspect of the BCDR so effectively; his work brings a forgotten era back to life.

Photographs on the opposite page, all W Robb:

Top: **On Easter Tuesday, 29th March 1932, 0-6-0 No 14 is emerging from the Gullet with the 2.30pm to Newcastle.**

Bottom left: **No 4 blasts her way through the Gullet on the 2.30pm excursion to Newcastle, on 16th July 1932**

Bottom right: **In 1945, one of the BCDR horseboxes is behind No 6 as she heads a down Newcastle train.**

Photographs on this page, all W Robb:

Top: **No 21, with the 4.25pm up train from Newcastle, approaches Comber on 4th July 1933. The leading vehicle is a 6-wheeled fish van.**

Centre right: **That 2.30pm to Newcastle, once again headed by No 14, bursts forth from Ballynichol Bridge on 16th May 1931.**

Bottom right: **...and again, with No 4 on 26th August 1933.**

Left: **Haycocks in the summer fields as No 14 approaches Ballynichol Bridge on an up morning goods in 1934.** William Robb

Below: **Part of the farm owned by the Robb family is on the left. No 26 is seen here on 12th July 1931, hauling the empty stock for an Orange Demonstration special. The leading van and goods and cattle wagon are provided for banners and band instruments.** William Robb

BALLYGOWAN

Opened with the Downpatrick Extension in 1858, Ballygowan never had more than a single platform on the down side. The original goods siding was on the opposite side of the line and included a cattle beach and a loading bank for the local stone traffic.

As part of the improvements required by the Regulation Act, Ballygowan was made a block post in 1896/7, but the passing loop was allowed to handle goods trains only. A goods siding and store were added on the down side, south of the station, in 1898.

Top: **Looking from the level crossing as No 21 and the 7pm up Newcastle train pause at the single platform on 4th July 1933. It is a scene full of 'County Down' detail and includes some of Culverwell's paling alongside the platform ramp .**
W Robb

Centre right: **This overall view of Ballygowan from the south shows the goods store and siding provided in 1898.**

Bottom right: **Diesel-electric locomotive No 2 pauses at Ballygowan on a Comber to Ballynahinch train on 12th January 1950.**

SAINTFIELD

This was the only intermediate station to be planned from the beginning as a passing place, though the loop and second platform were not ordered to be built until July 1859. At first, up and down trains used either platform indiscriminately. The goods yard at the south end was separated from the passenger station by a level crossing.

Left: **In the verdant County Down countryside, No 18 approaches Saintfield on the 10.50am down Newcastle train, on 9th July 1935.** W Robb

Below: **No 21 draws out over the level crossing in autumn sunshine with a Newcastle train on 21st September 1940.** W Robb

Top right: **Saintfield was the epitome of a rural station on the BCDR. It is now listed as an Historic Monument and it is to be hoped that, some day, it will return to the condition seen here on 21st April 1951. In this view from the station forecourt, Culverwell's Stationmaster's house is on the left. In the middle is Gray's station building of the 1850s in stone and brick. Unusually, the later signal cabin was built to match.**

Centre right: **Saintfield goods yard lay on the down side of the level crossing. The solid-looking goods store was one of the original structures. On 21st April 1951 it still contains a BCDR covered goods wagon, but weeds are beginning to reclaim the permanent way.**

Below: **Exchanging the tablet as No 4, on the 4.45pm Newcastle train, crosses an up service at Saintfield.** E S Russell

BALLYNAHINCH JUNCTION

Laid out according to the prevailing logic, the junction for Ballynahinch had one platform on the down side of the single line, used by what little local traffic there was, and on the up side, an island platform, not very wide, which allowed passengers to cross to and from the branch train in its bay.

In 1860, a carriage shed was put up in the apex of the junction; this became a locomotive shed for a while.

Despite its archaic layout, 'The Junction' was a block post and occasional long goods trains had to be parked on the branch, thereby impeding passengers to and from Ballynahinch. There was sufficient local goods traffic to warrant a cheaply-built goods store made of corrugated iron on a short siding on the down side of the main line.

When the line closed, the UTA was obliged to provide a special bus service to serve this isolated community.

Top: **Platform furniture at the Junction. Untypically, the station nameboard was painted – screw-on cast iron lettering was more common on the BCDR. One imagines that the expression of company loyalty exemplified by a concrete casting of the coat-of-arms was done for the best kept station awards which generated fierce competition.** E S Russell

Centre: **This close-up of the Junction footbridge, down-end water tank and signals emphasises the rather weird layout here. The uncomfortably narrow island platform ruled out provision of umbrella roofing and the only real cure was a complete remodelling of the station, though the nettle was never grasped. The signal arms are plainly of LNWR style made in corrugated metal and the wooden posts have flat caps in North Western fashion. In the distance can be seen the 1857 water tower, once fed by a steam pump and then by wind-power. This view was taken on 21st April 1951.**

Bottom left: **On the 2.20pm Newcastle, the veteran No 27 is entering the Junction in June 1949.** E.S.Russell

Top right: **The Ballynahinch train in its bay platform, in the early days of diesel-electric power. No D1 (later renumbered 2) still has the new look about her. The two-coach set has been given electric battery heating as D1 has no means of supplying steam heat. The coaches are Ashbury brake-third No 134, of 1893 and Metropolitan first-second No 113 built in 1891.** W Robb

Centre right: **A rare glimpse of the Great Southern Railway's 2-4-2T No 430, a former Dublin & South Eastern locomotive, on the branch set on 16th April 1941. This wartime loan came as a surprise. Seldom seen or heard in Belfast, No 430 had a clear soprano whistle noticeably different to the BCDR mezzo-soprano and the GNR contralto (to say nothing of the NCC coloratura 'pipsqueak'). The branch train is now loaded to three coaches. On the left are some of the banner signals introduced after a derailment in 1917, in order to cover extra shunting movements. The Junction signalbox's frame had run out of spare levers for conventional signals.** W Robb

Below: **With the return of peace in 1945, the rebuilt 2-4-0 No 6 was less in demand for main line duties and it is sad to see her back to being spare engine on the Ballynahinch branch. Diesel-electric No 2's indifferent performance meant that No 6 would have plenty of mileage ahead of her.** Drew Donaldson

Above and below: **These two photographs, taken in June 1949, convey a wealth of information, including the loading of the 2pm up Newcastle train. At each end there are 4-wheeled fitted or piped vans; a County Down horsebox is among three NCC covered wagons at the front, while a further three NCC vans at the rear are tailed by a BCDR 'blocked' (vacuum braked) goods and cattle van in bauxite red.**

We are not sure whether rules weren't bent that day to allow such a formation. In the first picture, above, taken on the south side of the road overbridge, the goods siding turnout on the far side may just be discerned. The goods shed itself is concealed by the train. A loading gauge standing on empty ballast on the right marks the site of the 1860 carriage shed. The actual siding lasted longer but had

been lifted by 1939. In the second picture, No 4 has come to a stand between the platforms; there is a good view of the Junction cabin, built high for visibility above the road bridge, and the third on the BCDR to carry its name. On the left, the branch train with diesel-electric No 2, makes its connection. Both E S Russell

BALLYNAHINCH

The plans for this station (which included a small engine shed that was never built) show very clearly that it was designed to be a through station with a middle road, like Comber. This became the engine run-round. A pleasant two-storey station building lay alongside what was to have been the up platform, and the down platform became a loading dock known as the 'pork platform'. The branch engine was stabled in the goods store at first, then banished to the Junction for a period. An engine shed was eventually built, in 1896, on the down side of the line in the rock cutting outside the terminus. The all-over roof covering the three roads was a surprising addition at the same time. The platform verandah it displaced was re-erected at Comber.

Top right: **No 2, the Harlandic diesel-electric is coupling up to the branch set in noonday sunshine in June 1949. The formation, after the wartime boom, has reverted to two coaches, a six-compartment third and the brake first-second. The diesel is still in its 'invisible green' livery and appears never to have been repainted during its time on the BCDR.** E S Russell

Centre right: **The terminus on 12th February 1949 presents a very unified appearance, with de Witt Gray's stucco-faced station house (on the right) linked to the triple-gabled goods store by the train shed of 1896. On this day 2-4-0 No 6 was working the branch, but she is out of sight behind the photographer.**

Bottom: **This view, from the hillside through which the railway entered Ballynahinch, is full of detail. Note the little loading dock with its own lean-to shed outside the goods store. The vehicle with torpedo vents in the foreground is one of the 6-wheel bread vans. The most puzzling feature in this late '30s scene is the colossal amount of locomotive coal beside the coaling stage, seemingly more than enough for one steam engine working full-time on the branch – now nominally in the hands of the diesel. The local coal factors operated from a depot out of sight on the left. The compact terminus presents a compelling invitation to the modelling fraternity. In the background, the little hills of Down, as the Psalmist has it, '. . . rejoice on every side.'**
Author's collection

CROSSGAR

Following our brief excursion down the branch we return to the main line and leave Ballynahinch Junction to head south to the next station, Crossgar. In its final form, the layout at Crossgar was a mirror image of that at Saintfield, bar the level crossing. Again, one of the original stations on the extension, it received its passing loop and up platform in 1893. The signal cabin on the new platform was grouped with a waiting shed and covered subway approach, a nice composition repeated at Newtownards. Crossgar remains a photographic desert, the author's solitary picture being taken more than a year after closure.

Above: **Big 0-6-0 No 10 leaves the Junction on what is probably a down Saturday excursion to Newcastle. The photographer was standing on the Ballynahinch fork of the actual junction. The date is around 1938 and No 10 has been repainted in the new livery.** Drew Donaldson

Below: **Crossgar, looking northwards, on 21st April 1951. It is more than a year after closure. Country folk were well-behaved then, and vandalism was not obligatory – glass in the waiting shed and signal cabin on the up platform remains intact. The goods store and yard are behind the camera. There is a sheep pen alongside the yard headshunt, but the long cattle beach is out of sight on the extreme down side of the yard.**

DOWNPATRICK

Our coverage of the railway at Downpatrick reflects both how things were in the BCDR era and the scene today where this historic cathedral town is the base for Ireland's only operating preserved standard gauge railway.

The Loop Line, which enabled through trains to avoid a reversal at Downpatrick, diverged from the old main line at Downpatrick North Junction (about 53 chains short of the terminus), the latter swinging left, under the Cathedral hill, to terminate alongside Market Street, tolerably near the town centre. The Newcastle line trailed in to a scissors junction at the 'Home Cabin', where the goods sidings diverged to the right. Downpatrick Station consisted of a two-road passenger shed but only one platform. This was lengthened at the outer end of the shed. A bay was made alongside for DD&NR use; this was for the Ardglass branch trains from 1892. Both extended platform and bay were given umbrella roofing in 1897. The main line ended at a turntable (1886) and a single-road engine shed was built alongside the passenger shed in 1892. A new engine release road was laid round the back of the station at the same time. The old engine shed and turntable of 1859 were situated between goods yard and passenger station. The shed became part of a coal depot when vacated by BCDR engines. The station building, a single-storey structure with a central turret, was modified in the 1890s by giving it a second storey to act as the Stationmaster's residence, situated over the station entrance. Used latterly as the UTA bus station, it was demolished in the 1970s. The site is now covered by a supermarket.

Top: **Steam traction is seen again on part of the BCDR main line as 0-4-0 saddle tank No 2, built for use at Guinness' brewery in Dublin in 1919 and subsequently preserved by the Railway Preservation Society of Ireland, approaches the Loop Line platform with a train from the new station at Downpatrick.** Gerry Cochrane

Centre: **The rebuilt Loop Line platform at Downpatrick. In this view looking south, the line from Downpatrick is on the left, the actual loop line which enabled trains to run direct to Newcastle without reversing is that on the right of the picture.** Gerry Cochrane

Bottom: **At the reconstructed Downpatrick station, the Guinness tank is seen alongside ex-CIE diesel shunter E432. The bracket signals in the foreground are authentic BCDR specimens which were originally the starting signals for platforms 1 and 2 at Bangor Station. They are very similar to the starting signals at the BCDR Downpatrick terminus, seen on page 51.** Gerry Cochrane

Above: **Downpatrick passenger station in June 1949. The coaling stage is on the left. No 1 waits to depart on the 3.30pm to Newcastle, having exchanged Ardglass duties with No 27.** E S Russell

Below: **No 1 is getting away in fine style with the 3.30pm Newcastle train that began its journey behind No 27 as the 2.20pm from Belfast. A nice panoramic view of the terminus in June 1949, with Market Street in the right background.** E S Russell

Opposite page, top: **A general view of Downpatrick terminus in June 1949. The Ardglass branch set is at the platform to the right, and the engine shed – a less-imposing edifice than the 1859 shed – is on the extreme left of the picture.** E S Russell

On the Loop Line itself a platform was constructed in 1893. This was situated in the 'V'
between the Loop Line and the southbound
line leading out from the terminal station. A
canopy was provided at this platform in 1907
and a run-round siding was built off the line
leading to Downpatrick, in 1905.

The present day Downpatrick & Ardglass
Railway, a limited company with charitable status, was set up in 1985 and much has been
accomplished since that time. A new station
has been built on the approximate site of the
original terminal of 1859. It is a pleasant
Victorian pastiche incorporating the house for-
merly occupied by the manager of the town's
Gas Works, which was removed and rebuilt
from its original site on the other side of
Market Street. Track has been relaid from the
new station beyond the Loop Line platform
and past the site of the former South Junction.
A new platform has been built here, called King
Magnus' Halt, as it is close to the burial site of
this Viking king. In 1993 a canopy, resembling
the original, was built on the Loop Line platform. Several steam and diesel locomotives are
based at Downpatrick, as is a good selection of
rolling stock in various stages of restoration.
Among BCDR relics which have found sanctu-
ary here are the Royal Saloon dating from 1897
and a railmotor carriage of 1905 vintage.

Right: **Looking 'up' from the island
platform on 21st April 1951, the Ardglass
bay is at the left. In the background are the
cattle beach and outer end of goods yard.**

THE ARDGLASS RAILWAY

A Light Railway Order to enable this line to be constructed was made in September 1890, though in truth the only aspect of this branch that could be called light was the earthworks. New 80lb steel rails were laid, normal rolling stock worked over the line, and while motive power was usually of the smallest type owned by the Company, this ranged from 2-4-0ST, 0-4-2T and 2-4-2T engines to the standard 4-4-2 tank locomotives which were often seen on the branch.

Moreover, all the stations had block signalling until the economies of the 1920s. The diesel-electric engine No 28 worked the line, with much absenteeism, from 1937 to 1944. The two intermediate stations were Ballynoe (30 miles 2 chains from Belfast) and Killough (33 miles 65 chains), both with passing loops though the latter had only a single passenger platform. Ardglass (35 miles 19 chains) was given a bay platform. Not surprisingly, photographs of Ballynoe and Killough are scarce; this is a pity, for Culverwell and his assistant Morris designed handsome little stations for the Light Railway. Track layout diagrams for all three of the stations on the branch are shown opposite.

Top: **Passengers' view of Killough on 15th September 1949. This gives some idea of the 10 chain curve through the station, and the rustic construction of the cattle beach on its loop siding. The platform and station house are on the far side of the train.**

Photographs on the opposite page:

Centre: **The goods yard and store at Ardglass. Livestock traffic on the branch was at a low ebb in 1949, as the grassy state of the cattle beach shows. The building behind the goods store is one of the 'monstrous parasites' accommodating the activities of the NIRTB – referred to in the Introduction.**

Bottom: **Looking across the bay platform road at Ardglass, almost obscured by summer grass, No 27 is on branch line duty. She will be leaving for Downpatrick at 4.10pm and the train is scheduled as 'mixed', but no goods are on offer this June day in 1949. Ardglass station buildings were quite extensive; the two-storey building on the right was the Stationmaster's house. E S Russell**

Photographs on this page:

Top: **No 1 has brought in the 12.05pm mixed train from Downpatrick. Its freight load on this particular day, 15th September 1949, is no more than a 6-wheeled bread van and a goods and cattle wagon.**

Centre: **Ardglass from the dead-end, as No 1 runs around her train which will leave for Downpatrick at 1.10pm, making a connection with what has now become the 2.25pm from Belfast. No 1 will run bunker first. The Ardglass table saw little use except by tender engines on excursion trains.; its provision in the first place had been a requirement of the Board of Trade.**

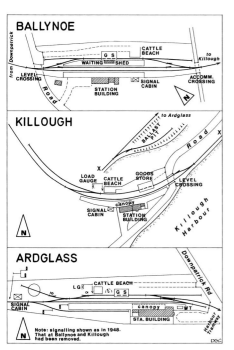

End of the line at Ardglass. Beyond the mound in the background, the tarred-over remains of the harbour tramway still lie beneath the public road to Ardglass Harbour. The three-track layout shown on the diagram was taken out by the BCDR in the last months of independent existence.

TULLYMURRY

The first station at Tullymurry dealt with goods and passenger traffic at the same platform. It had been opened in 1871 by the DD&NR without Board of Trade sanction. There was a level crossing at the Belfast end, replaced by a road overbridge when the old station was closed.

The establishment of an Army camp at nearby Ballykinlar led to the construction of the second station on a new site about a quarter-mile south of the original one. This had a single platform on the up side with a neat red and blue brick station building and Stationmaster's house alongside the Downpatrick to Dundrum road. A bijou signal cabin in matching brick was built on the platform, gable end-on to the line. There was a goods yard but no passing loop. The new Tullymurry station opened for traffic on 2nd August 1897. Goods sidings were extended for military traffic in the First World War and the Second World War again brought much business to the yard.

From September 1914, troop trains used Ballykinlar Halt, a bare platform on the up side of the line at 32 miles 10 chains.

Top: **Tullymurry: a roadside view eleven years after cessation of services. Realignment has brought the Downpatrick road perilously close but the attractive station is still remarkably complete, and has acquired petrol pumps in the forecourt! Even the yard crane is still there.**

Centre left: **The platform side is less attractive now, though all the Culverwell-Morris hallmarks are still there. The buildings were in red Belfast brick, with decorative courses and hood-mouldings in blue Staffordshire brick.**

Bottom left: **Tullymurry signal cabin, purpose-made for its situation, was unique on the BCDR, and like the rest of the station would have been a nice subject for modelling.**

DUNDRUM

Dundrum Bay, although a place of treacherous sand-bars – for Brunel's *Great Britain* went aground there in 1846 – is a safe haven for smaller vessels, and the harbour developed by the Marquess of Downshire provided the Newcastle line with its best source of goods traffic. The East Downshire Steamship Company imported coal through Dundrum and distributed it by rail to its depots in Ballynahinch, Downpatrick, Newcastle and Banbridge. It enlivened the railway scene by using its own wagons from the earliest days up to closure of the Newcastle line.

Dundrum station was sandwiched between the Newcastle road and the harbour, lack of foresight resulting in a cramped and inconvenient layout. Needless to say, it was not possible to cross passenger trains at Dundrum. A siding parallel to the running line served the tall goods warehouse that was an original feature. A series of wagon turntables sent the empty wagons on to the quay for loading. There was a good outward traffic in potatoes, did the spuds ballast the empty colliers? The BCDR did the best it could in the Regulation Act work, with a loop siding on the landward side for the cattle beach.

Later, Culverwell designed a new station on the down side of the harbour crossing where there was more room, but it was never built. Dundrum had been the railhead for Castlewellan and when that line opened most of the goods traffic melted away. Strangely enough, a timber-built goods shed of Culverwellian appearance existed for many years on the up side of the line at the site of the proposed new station. This was the warehouse of the North of Ireland Produce Company, who had a private siding from 1915 to 1924.

For all its disadvantages, there was still considerable charm about Dundrum station.

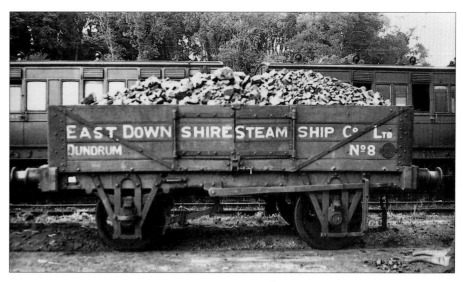

Above: **The East Downshire Steamship Company owned a maximum of 20 wagons, painted light grey with yellow lettering. There were 3-plank and 4-plank varieties though all were rated as 10-ton capacity. They were registered with the BCDR, carrying the standard Railway Clearing House plates. The split-spoked wheels had sheet-metal covering to discourage spragging,** but No 8, seen at Downpatrick in 1949, has acquired solid steel wheels with holes allowing just that. Apart from the outside axle-guards, they had no BCDR features. The corner plates and self-contained buffers were especially untypical of BCDR practice. These wagons were normally not seen north of Ballynahinch, except when going for repairs at Queen's Quay shops.

Centre right: **Dundrum station building was in a cramped position between Main Street and the BCDR main line ...**

Bottom right: **...and there was just enough room for that main line and a siding (terminating in a wagon turntable) between the quayside warehouse and the single passenger platform. Both views were recorded on 15th September 1963.**

NEWCASTLE

The old DD&NR station of 1869 was almost completely transformed in the successive remodellings of 1899 and 1905. The former, in association with the Slieve Donard Hotel construction, involved making a new goods yard on the west side of the passenger platform, demolishing the old goods store that would have been an unwelcome neighbour for a luxury hotel and providing a new arrival platform in its place, complete with entrance into the hotel grounds. The DD&NR engine shed was lengthened at the same time.

The second phase was to build a new single-storey station in red brick beyond the buffer stops, expensively roofed with Westmorland green slates. There was a lofty, glazed iron canopy at the entrance and the 1899 platform was given a verandah covering. The dominant feature of the new station, spoiling the overall effect, was a squat clock tower with copper-clad spire, grossly disproportionate. It was as if a much taller building had sunk into the ground under its own weight. Once inside however, the flower-bedecked concourse had a wonderfully cosmopolitan atmosphere, with clock-faces at each platform entrance giving times of train departures for Dublin on the left and Belfast on the right.

The engine shed was again enlarged to become a twin-gabled two road building, GNR locomotives occupying what was effectively a separate shed walled off from County Down premises.

The old station building remained, much altered, fronting a platform that was always unroofed. The adjoining 'Railway Pavilion', similar in function to that at Donaghadee, was built in the 1890s. A feature of the goods yard was the East Downshire coal depot, a two-level building where loaded wagons were winched up an incline to be discharged into bins for grading and bagging. The coal siding had a loop to separate full and empty wagons.

One further task for the BCDR engineer was to relay Newcastle station throat, simplifying an interesting layout. The junction for Castlewellan was immediately outside the yard, worked by the Newcastle cabin. Parallel with the BCDR main line was the carriage siding, almost half a mile long, where excursion trains were parked end to end during the summer season.

Right: **Evening mists gather over the Mournes as No 18 shunts the stock of the up 'Golfers'. She is propelling it from the Warren siding towards No 1 platform. The train is formed as follows: 6-wheel passenger van (second series); 6-wheel second third; bogie first-second; bogie brake third. Bringing up the rear is first class saloon No 153, otherwise known as the Golfers' Saloon. It is a Saturday in August 1941. Devotees of County Down rolling stock will find this significant, for there are continuous lower footboards on the two compartment bogie coaches, a feature that will have disappeared entirely in the following year. At the extreme right of the picture, another engine can just be seen outside the shed, the twin gables of which are visible above the last two coaches.** W Robb

Bottom right: **Running well behind time, 0-6-0 No 14 rattles into Newcastle with the 12.50pm down train, which was routed by Downpatrick. There, No 14 ran round her train without using the turntable and saved a few precious minutes at the expense of the enginemens' comfort. At Newcastle, No 14's train is signalled into No 2 platform; the run round crossover at the end of No 1 cannot be used owing to the presence of the Golfers' Saloon against the buffer stops.**

Right: **The 10.45am Great Northern train from Belfast arrives headed by 4-4-0 No 200 at 1.30pm, some 29 minutes late. On the GNR the up direction was the opposite to that on the BCDR, thus GNR trains ran down to Belfast whereas County Down ones went up to the city. She had turned and was away again at 1.45pm, an 'on-time' departure. This engine is one of the first batch of class 'U' built in 1915 and much used on secondary lines with a restricted axle-loading. When a further five engines (the 'Counties', painted in the lovely lined-out blue livery), were supplied by Beyer Peacock in 1948, the original five received the same treatment. They were named after Ulster lakes, No 200 becoming *Lough Melvin*. The west flank of the original engine shed is seen on the right.**

Above: **A signalman's view of the Newcastle terminus. It will be seen that there was plenty of room for development but the need never arose. The 'Railway Pavilion' is in the centre background. The date is 26th March 1955 and the Great Northern service will be withdrawn in a matter of weeks, leaving Newcastle without a train service of any kind.**

Right: **Stock movements in this small terminus appeared to have been well planned in advance – or were they? Here, No 14 has retrieved the Saloon from the end of No 1 platform and is about to place it at the end of the middle road. After this, the locomotive will shunt the coaches of the 12.50pm into the goods yard and eventually into the Warren siding.**

Above: **On 10th September 1949 No 1 has brought in the 1.50pm train from Belfast. She will run round and park her coaches in the goods yard before picking her way across the double slip and finding refuge in the locomotive yard.**

Centre left: **Still the day-trippers come. The signalman watches No 17 coming in smartly on the 2.35pm ex-Belfast. The leading vehicle is former railmotor No 1, now brake-open third No 59. It is only a week out of the paint shop in the new UTA livery of Brunswick green and has been borrowed from the Holywood shuttle to strengthen the 2.35. Note the two water tanks and goods yard starting signals on the left. Beyond the cabin is visible one of the two NCC caravan coaches introduced by the UTA.**

Left: **Here is No 1 at rest and taking water outside Newcastle shed.**

Above left: **The working timetable showed a pick-up goods leaving for Downpatrick at 3.40pm on Saturdays. This was a turn for No 14; the photographer was hoping for some East Downshire empties but that day it was only the engine and a brake van. It was a melancholy hint of declining traffic, we thought, but two months later the same working featured 0-6-0 No 4 with a very respectable train.**

Above right: **In the midst of all the activity of a busy summer Saturday, large 4-4-2T No 16 arrived on a military special to Ballykinlar from Belfast. Having run round its empty stock at Newcastle, No 16 filled its tanks and took its train back to the city without further ado.**

Below: **GNR 'UG' class 0-6-0 No 79 had brought in the 1.40pm from Belfast**

(Great Victoria Street) and will leave again at 4.55pm. In this instance No 79 is about to go to the turntable. It is a tight fit between the BCDR stock and the switch for the table road. The Golfers' Saloon and the rest of the stock in the Warren siding, beyond the GNR locomotive's tender, will be reversed into No 1 platform to form the 5.45pm up train to Queen's Quay.

Above, right: **This shunting signal at Newcastle permitted backing movements into both passenger platforms and the middle road.**

Below: **These miniature semaphores produced by the Railway Signal Company of Liverpool were widely used by the BCDR for shunting movements in single-arm and multiple-arm modes.**

Top: **On 10th September 1949, No 21 heads the 5.45pm Belfast train at the spacious No 1 platform that was added in 1899. The notice directing patrons to the Slieve Donard Hotel is prominent. The verandah front of the original Newcastle station (seldom featuring in photographs) would have been lost if the Great Northern had insisted on proper umbrella roofing for its platform on the right. Perhaps they refused to pay the BCDR for such a luxury for their passengers?** W Robb

Above: **There were still excursions to Newcastle at the tail end of that last summer of the BCDR main line, and trains like this Great Northern special would still be coming here for another six years or so. UG class 0-6-0 No 78 and train are parked on the goods yard headshunt this Saturday afternoon, 10th September 1949. No 78 is standing on iron bridge rail a lot older than the Downpatrick & Newcastle Railway itself. You could also find the odd upright of Barlow rail holding up notice boards.**

CASTLEWELLAN

Castlewellan was at first glance a typical GNR wayside station. Its buildings, including goods shed, signal cabin and waiting rooms were timber framed and sheeted in that company's distinctive style, while the Stationmaster's house, in polychrome brick, was also pure Great Northern, as was the signalling. That it was a joint station is often overlooked. R M Arnold attributed the use of a subway to BCDR influence, though the station was on an embankment between two road underbridges, leaving no real alternative. It was also at the top of a 1 in 70 incline from Newcastle, probably the steepest on the BCDR, a line that had not much use for gradient posts. The climb eased to a mere 1 in 300 through the station before steepening again to a summit at Leitrim four miles further on. Castlewellan station was actually in the hamlet of Annsboro, below the hilltop town. The goods yard on the west side (BCDR down side, GNR up) had three sidings and a long headshunt at the GNR end. From this the BCDR built a private siding for Murland & Company's Greenvale Bleach Works on the Castlewellan road. As this end of the headshunt was on GNR land, the BCDR paid half its cost in return for a rebate on tolls. A siding off the (BCDR) up loop was laid on to BCDR land where a turntable was placed at the insistence of the Board of Trade, this being a terminus for County Down trains. The table saw little use

and was disconnected in 1930. Maintenance of the joint station alternated between the GNR and BCDR on a yearly basis. It is said also that the staff wore each company's uniform on alternate years.

Above: **This view, in County Down terms, is looking 'up' to Newcastle. Everything in sight is pure GNR, from the W H Mills designed signal cabin to the station buildings on the right.**

Below: **In the opposite direction, Murland's mill chimney dominates the skyline and the goods yard occupies the middle ground. The subway entrances are under the station verandah on the left and beside the waiting shed on the right. Both views were taken on 25th May 1957, after closure. An air of decay has descended, glass has been smashed and palings have been stolen, the latter probably for use as firewood.**

THE BANGOR BRANCH

Above: **A closer look at the single-storeyed station building shows also how the footbridge access from the up platform was arranged. The buildings were quite distinctive and unlike any others on the system.**

SYDENHAM

The second of the intermediate stations on the Holywood branch originated as a mere stopping place without platform, taking its name from the townland of Ballymisert. A BCDR shareholder offered land for a permanent station in 1851 and a platform was built. Suburban Belfast was developing rapidly and the more sophisticated name of Sydenham was adopted for the district. The station took this appelation in 1856. Brick station buildings on the up platform were built by the BHBR in the 1870s. Sydenham was a block post until automatic signalling was introduced in the 1920s, the signal cabin also was on the up platform. There was a plate-girder footbridge at the up end. A level crossing was opened for military and later for public use during the Second World War, land reclamation having allowed development of Shorts' aircraft factory and the adjacent Royal Naval Aircraft yard. The station now serves Belfast Harbour Airport, which has been developed on the site. A short distance down the line, a trailing crossover existed until 1942: it had proved useful in reversing trains during the previous year's 'blitz'.

Top left: **The Belfast, Holywood & Bangor stationmaster's house, seen from Inverary Drive. The footbridge was designed for public use and consequently had a double stairway on each side.**

Top right: **Sydenham cabin was typically Culverwellian in detail and markedly similar to the signal box at Craigavad.**

Above: **A general view of Sydenham, looking north-east. The level crossing was in the foreground. The signal cabin on the up platform had no further use when this crossing was abolished, but was retained as a store. Everything except the platforms and footbridge were swept away in the 'sixties.**

TILLYSBURN

This was the second station in the locality, opened by the BHBR in 1880. The first Tillysburn was about a quarter of a mile nearer Holywood, where the railway crossed the stream of the same name, and was accessible only by a footpath along its bank. There were several large houses in the vicinity and the rail service commenced on 1st November 1848 on a surprisingly limited basis, being available only to season-ticket holders, their relatives and friends – and tickets had to be purchased in Belfast! BHBR trains stopped calling in 1877.

The company was persuaded to relocate the station, the new Tillysburn having a laneway to the nearby Holywood road, and gas lighting into the bargain. The BCDR provided a footbridge between platforms when the railmotor service to Holywood was instituted in 1905. Towards the end of the First World War it was decided to make Tillysburn a block post and the new cabin, on the down platform, and signals were brought into use on 1st July 1918. It had the shortest life of any BCDR cabin, closing in early 1925.

Road competition brought about the closure of Tillysburn itself in May 1931. Wartime petrol shortages were responsible for its reopening in 1941 when the 'Holywood Motors' called there once more. Tillysburn continued to be served until 1945. The pathetic ruins of the waiting sheds and cabin on the two substantial platforms lingered on for many years along with its almost modern footbridge, which was dismantled by the UTA and re-erected at Mount Halt on the Larne line, on the other side of Belfast Lough.

Top right: **Close to the main road but surrounded by dismal, half-reclaimed sloblands, Tillysburn did not attract photographers. All we can show you is the plate-girder footbridge, good enough to be salvaged for re-use in its new location at Mount Halt on the Larne line near Carrickfergus. The halt was built for the use of Courtaulds' employees and closed when the factory ceased production. It was photographed on 17th April 1963.**

KINNERGAR HALT

This was one of the halts that were built for the Holywood railmotors in 1905; others were at Ballymacarrett and Victoria Park, but they were featureless and almost devoid of furnishings, though their platforms were lengthened in later years to enable them to be served by the Bangor trains. Kinnegar had the distinction of

a footbridge, a lattice one, and was situated at an accommodation crossing giving access to the War Office rifle ranges on the bleak and windswept warrens. It was the first of the halts to close, in 1957.

Above: **We began this review of the BCDR at Belfast, where a 1951 view of the 'Bridge of Signals' includes the unlikely-looking Ganz railcar. Before this was purchased,** clearance trials had to be undertaken all over the UTA system. On the BCDR section, the longest coach, ex-railmotor No 173, was fitted with templates on the bogies and propelled over the entire County Down line by a 'bogie tank' and with saloon No 53 leading. Here it clears Kinnegar on the up journey; providing a glimpse of the halt and its footbridge on the left of the picture. By the time the Ganz itself arrived, only the Bangor line remained. Joe Lloyd

HOLYWOOD

Holywood was a station that has seen more than its share of rebuilding, to say nothing of demolition, in its 150-year history. The permanent station house, built in 1850, served its purpose until removed by the UTA as a first step in reducing a considerable railway station to a bare, unstaffed halt. The original terminus was at street level in Redburn Square. The BHBR curved down from Marino on the seaward side, crossing the foreshore approach on a low bridge and continuing to fall until it joined the BCDR by a double junction at the Belfast end of the yard. A platform was built on the up side of the line, referred to in early days as the 'high level platform'. The old station was left on a spur and Holywood short workings continued to terminate here. The BHBR covered its through platform with an interesting timber canopy having an elaborate coffered ceiling and a gable at the Belfast end with the company initials in fretwork.

The economics of the 1950s demanded that it all be razed to the ground. The monogram was acquired by the Belfast Transport Museum and has subsequently gone to the splendid new museum at Cultra, though at the time of writing, it is not on display to the public.

The track between Belfast and Holywood was eventually doubled before the 1884 take-over and the station was remodelled by Berkeley Wise in 1886. He added the down platform, giving it a segmental section canopy roofed in corrugated iron, and built a tall signal cabin at the Bangor end. A middle road through the station which was useful to shunt local trains clear of the main line was also provided. A bay platform on the up side saw only occasional use after the introduction of railmotors and the later push-and-pull trains which used the down platform for arrivals and departures. A sizeable goods yard occupied the 1848 station ground.

The construction of a section of dual carriageway of the A2, bypassing the town, has cut a swathe through the former goods yard and isolated Holywood station from the town.

Opposite page top: **A view from the up platform on 6th September 1949 as No 22 races through with the 1.17pm Bangor express. The middle road is still in use; note how narrow is the 'six-foot way' on either side. Berkeley Wise's umbrella roof on the down platform, corrugated iron coated with tar, was not one of his best works. Holywood gasworks in the background was a good customer of the BCDR but about this time a gas main was laid between Belfast and Holywood. The works closed though a gasholder was retained. A five-arm shunting signal controlled movements across the station. On the left hand side of the platform, in the foreground, was the up bay.**

Opposite page bottom: **The date is 6th September 1949. No 20 has used the middle road to run round its train and waits for the up wrong-line starter to clear for the return trip to Belfast. Lunch-time Holywood commuters have the unaccustomed comfort of four Northern Counties bogie coaches, half the 8-coach set provided for the two most important trains, the 8.20am up and 5.35pm down, when the UTA took control. We thought we were in clover, but the sardine-tin DMUs were to take over in a few years.**

This page top: **Another lunch-time scene at the down platform, but the rolling stock brought in by No 12 is the more familiar 'motor' set, no longer push-and-pull, of course. The leading coach is a brake ended first-second composite. Wise's tall signal cabin on the right straddled the way out. Passengers came and went, oblivious of the locking-frame above their heads. The train is the 1.20pm down, on 9th March 1949.**

Above: **Holywood goods yard was still functioning on 24th March 1949. The BHBR monogram on the station gable is just obscured by the masonry wall on the left. This was once the seaward boundary of the 1848 station and the bay platform road lies behind it.**

Right: **Holywood signal cabin was to remain a bastion of manual operation long after 21st November 1932, when automatic signalling of the Bangor line had been completed. Berkeley Wise's design was an undoubted forerunner of the many cabins built under his regime on the BNCR and the Midland Railway (NCC), with its overhanging eaves and hipped roof. This is a late view after removal of the third road, the Holywood down platform will soon be completely bare.**

MARINO

Marino was a Belfast, Holywood & Bangor Railway station dating from around 1869. When the doubling between Holywood and Craigavad was completed in late 1900, Marino was given waiting rooms, a booking office and other offices on the new up platform. The single-storey BHBR station house on the down platform acquired an extra storey and became the stationmaster's house, with a waiting room attached.

Top left: **Taken from the site of the newer station buildings provided when the line was doubled, the photograph shows the original BHBR station house as enlarged by the BCDR. The wheel turned full circle and before the whole building passed into private hands, all the public had was a waiting shed at one end. The date is 2nd September 1968.**

CULTRA

The single-platform station of 1865 was on the down side of the line. A clause in the BHBR Act called for a station, 'of ornamental character', in keeping with the high-class villas being built by Charles Lanyon on the Cultra estate. Lanyon, who laid out the BHBR, was one of the last great engineer-architects and chairman of the BHBR after 1873. He was knighted in 1868. Lanyon's office designed a little station in the Tudor fashion, made of brick with stone dressings. Damaged by a malicious fire in 1896, it was replaced by a much larger building based on the new Tullymurry station, but with a red-tiled roof. Cultra got a covered footbridge when the line was doubled, the only one on the system, which shows the regard the Company had for Cultra subscribers. There were new buildings on the up platform in the same style.

Centre left and bottom: **Cultra was reduced to Halt status in 1934 and given a purpose-made addition to the standard nameboard. At this time the 1896 station building became a private dwelling, while the footbridge and the tiled-roof waiting shed on the up platform were dispensed with. Photographed on 9th November 1957 during the long period of closure before Cultra became the recognised stopping place for the Ulster Folk & Transport Museum, which as well as being served by the station, has a connection off the down line right into the railway gallery. The standard gauge exhibits were moved to the museum by means of this siding.**

CRAIGAVAD

Craigavad was a passing place from its opening in 1865, the only one in BHBR days between Holywood and Bangor. The station building was in red brick, having an affinity with the larger one at Bangor. Both were two-storeyed on the up side of the line, the ground floor being against the railway embankment.

The local post office was situated in this building, being accessible from the platform and managed by the stationmaster.

After the doubling of the Bangor line, trailing crossovers were laid at each end of Craigavad station and were useful in reversing those of the 'Holywood motors' that were extended to Craigavad at peak hours.

A goods platform and siding were provided behind the down platform in later years.

Top left: **Here is Craigavad station building after closure, as seen from the approach road. The ground-floor dwelling is still occupied.**

Above left: **A platform view after closure: Craigavad Post Office was at the right-hand end of the building and the wall-mounted letter box is still visible. The Post Office moved to a shop on the Bangor road when the station closed and its railway-style notice board went with it. After withdrawal of regular services Craigavad continued to be used by occasional troops of Scouts and Guides, who had camp sites in the neighbourhood.**

Above right: **The Sykes Banner automatic signals used between Holywood and Bangor were mounted on a variety of salvaged semaphore posts. This is the Craigavad down starter seen on 9th November 1957.**

Top right: **The signal cabin on the up platform was generally similar to that at Sydenham. The nameboard was added by the UTA.**

Below: **There was no independent subway between the platforms at Craigavad, and this long-winded notice on the down side directed departing travellers to the public roadway that passed under the line at the Belfast end. There is a noticeable lack of standardisation among the cast-iron letters. 9th November 1957.**

HELENS BAY

The showpiece of the Bangor line, built at the expense of the Marquess of Dufferin and Ava, was originally named after this nobleman's residence at Clandeboye and connected to it by a three-mile carriage drive. The latter had two road overbridges and an under bridge, passing under the BHBR to a courtyard linked to the private waiting room in the Scottish Baronial style station by a covered staircase. In 1885, with a select garden suburb being developed around the station, Clandeboye was renamed Helen's Bay in honour of the Marchioness.

Helens Bay – the apostrophe was seldom used – became popular with day trippers to the extent that an excursion platform was built on the goods siding of 1887 at the Bangor end of the station. The temptation to use this siding to cross trains was too great; the Board of Trade ticked off the BCDR for this and a proper passing loop and up platform were added in 1894.

When the Bangor line through Helens Bay was doubled in 1902, the goods siding was retained, and older commuters will recall the sickening crunch as down expresses hit the facing points at 60mph. Helens Bay was given a trailing crossover at each end and like Craigavad had an up 'wrong line' starting signal for trains turning back there.

Above: **Henry Casserley's photograph of 17th April 1948 fortunately shows Helens Bay in its complete form. The 'candle-snuffer' spire, just visible over the roof-ridge, and the glazing over the subway stairs would be gone in another year. The small parcels office (right foreground) had been the first signal box – note the gap for rodding in the platform wall. Culverwell's standard waiting shed on the up platform was to be halved in length. The strange piece of masonry in front of the banner signal is part of the Marquess's battlemented under-bridge.**

Left: **A closer view of the station building, a coronet and DA monogram may be seen on the gable in due deference to the station's noble patron of former years. The date is 19th November 1966.**

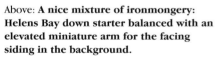

Above: **A nice mixture of ironmongery: Helens Bay down starter balanced with an elevated miniature arm for the facing siding in the background.**

Top right: **Helens Bay in the wet month of July 1965, with one of the last steam excursions from the GNR section. There would be no more of these after the erstwhile Belfast Central line was severed later in the year, isolating the Bangor branch from the rest of the Irish Railway network for over ten years.**

Above centre: **One of the older type of BCDR trespass notice at Helens Bay. The facing connection from the down line is seen on the right of the picture.**

Bottom right: **The signal cabin, showing signs of neglect in 1966. By this time it is no more than a ground frame for the up crossover and wrong-line starter, and the facing siding at the down end.**

CARNALEA

Carnalea station began as a small timber platform on the up side of the line. Its business was conducted from the body of a 4-wheeled passenger brake van with a 'birdcage' lookout. BHBR van No 2 had disappeared from the stock returns in 1873; this might point to a date for the station opening but other evidence indicates that trains began calling there in 1877. A short distance from the sea, Carnalea soon gained popularity and the surrounding area became a notable centre for week-end bungalows. The BCDR built a proper station of the Tullymurry pattern in 1897, complete with passing loop. The first portion of double track on the branch was Carnalea to Bangor, opened in June 1898. Carnalea also had the means of turning back trains, but this practice was discontinued as headways decreased. Carnalea cabin was closed in May 1926, being re-opened seasonally until automatic signalling was introduced in November 1932.

Top: **A simplified version of the standard nameboard.**

Centre: **The 1897 station building. The stationmaster's house has been sold and fenced off. November 1966.**

Below: **This attractive poster at Carnalea featured on many BCDR hoardings. Spoken of with affection by those fond of 'the hard stuff', Old Comber whiskey has long vanished from liquor stores.**

Above: **Carnalea down platform had one of Culverwell's waiting sheds. The rapid disappearance of these features makes one inclined to think that maintenance had** been neglected down the years and it may not have been just a ploy to reduce the rateable valuation. The photograph was taken on 15th September 1956.

BANGOR WEST HALT

The provision of a halt on the western outskirts of Bangor had been under consideration for several years, becoming a reality on 1st January 1928. The two 600ft platforms had ramped access from Bryansburn Road which crossed the line there. A timber booking office and waiting room on the up platform was in charge of a halt keeper; a small wooden waiting shed served the down platform. The 'Halt' grew in popularity and all Bangor expresses, up and down, were scheduled to stop there.

Right: **This 1956 view from the down platform entrance includes all the facilities as described, and electric light has arrived, complete with heavy 1950s concrete posts.**
Stations UK

Above: **Included to show what open country still existed between Bangor West and Bangor, even in 1960, the spire of Bangor Abbey and wooded Castle Park are seen across the fields. The accommodation path in the foreground led from the Halt to the Belfast road. The 'U class' 4-4-0 is on a returning excursion. The former No 196** *Lough Gill*, **it is still in GNR blue but has been renumbered 64 by the UTA.**

Centre right: **Recorded at Bangor West on 8th September 1957: Burgoyne's Ophir Rich Empire Wine is another long-gone tipple, advertised in coloured enamel on sheet-metal.**

Right: **These rectangular trespass notices were introduced in 1922. Chatams Limited of Tipton in Staffordshire, supplied 422 such plates to the BCDR.**

BANGOR

Behind Lanyon's cleverly designed terminal building on Abbey Street, the BHBR had handled its increasing passenger traffic on a single brick-paved platform, its goods in a short bay, and not much else except the engine run round. With many other irons in the fire, it was 1891 before the BCDR had commenced the long-needed remodelling. The first step was a third platform on the down side combined with shifting the buffer stops several feet nearer Belfast. A passenger shed at the rear of the brick station building sheltered the platforms and a large concourse behind the buffers, led on to a new station approach facing Dufferin Avenue where it met Main Street. A goods store and two sidings flanked the bay platform

(No 1), conveniently accessible from Abbey Street. Later, room was found for two long carriage sidings on the edge of the goods yard, trailing into the up main line just short of the overbridge carrying Brunswick Road across the line. Beyond here was another relic of the BHBR, the Upper Yard where a facing siding diverged left to serve the engine shed and turntable, the BCDR removed the latter to Donaghadee. There was also a curious gated siding which in our time had no obvious purpose except to harbour occasional permanent way wagons. The signal cabin was on the down side of the line adjacent to the impressive scissors crossover that gave access to and from all passenger platforms.

The layout worked well, but the station's importance was belittled by an overall meanness of size and finish. The spacious Newcastle terminus completed a few years after Bangor would never see anything like the volume of

traffic handled by the north Down station 12 months in the year.

Culverwell's passenger shed was cheaply built, all timber and felt, supported by what was known as a 'Belfast roof', an economical way of using short lengths of timber in laminated trusses. Either end of this curved roof was masked by the engineer's characteristic vertically planked gables, that on the street facade being emblazoned with the company's title in shaded block capitals. Below this was a rather scrappy elevation in horizontal sheeting, off-centre to allow for an opening for mails and luggage. It could be a draughty place at times.

By the early 1940s the all-over roof had decayed to the extent of requiring demolition back to the ticket barrier, leaving a gap between the platform canopies and the concourse, which was not filled until peace returned, when the remainder was replaced by a steel-framed pitched roof.

Left: **Photographed on 15th January 1950, Sir Charles Lanyon's terminal building, facing onto Abbey Street, is within days of being lost forever under a horrible jazz-modern facade as contractors commence work on an integrated rail and bus station. There are heaps of aggregate behind the stationmaster's garden fence and his house, along with the goods yard, has already vanished. However, we cannot blame the poor old UTA for everything - the BCDR had previously vandalised Lanyon's frontage with poster boards.**

Below: **A view from the 'barrier' end of platform 2 on 2nd June 1952 shows how the gap left by demolition of the train shed had been filled. A series of reinforced concrete cantilevered stanchions were cast in the goods yard and dropped one by one into place by the Adelaide breakdown crane of the GNR. This was during the post-war working-agreement between the companies.**

Right: **If ever a train was ignored by enthusiasts, this is it. Early on each weekday morning a modest freight arrived in Bangor. Here is the return working at around seven in the evening. No 19 shunts her train before departure but still has to marshal the brake van at the rear. In the background are the houses in Abbey Street and behind them the leafy demesne of Bangor Castle. It is early summer 1946.**

Centre right: **The 7.25pm up train departs from No 3 platform in charge of the renumbered 216 on 23rd June 1950. Note that the two carriage sidings on the right have been slewed over violently to make room for the new bus garage. The times are changing, a BCDR 7-compartment third on the siding has been newly painted green, matching its second class companion. The straight-sided bogie at the other end is an ex-NCC composite purchased in 1943. It will soon be joined by several more of the same ilk as the more modern LMS stock goes to Duncrue Street works for conversion to diesel railcars.**

Bottom: **There were no less than three excursions to Bangor from GNR stations on 23rd June 1950 (a week-day). The second of these is leaving for home, and is formed of eleven BCDR 6-wheelers with a GNR bogie at each end. The leading one is a mouth-watering specimen – GNR No 397 – one of the four surviving flat-roofed bogie coaches, of class F10, a first-second composite with luggage compartment, built in 1892. The train engine is ex-BCDR No 218.**

Top: **Between them, these two pictures by Eric Russell admirably record Bangor terminus as it was, before smitten by the hand of change. We guess that he had travelled by bus from Donaghadee after capturing the scene there on 6th June 1949. The first picture shows most of the terminal facilities in somewhat sharp perspective, the outer platform awnings and the steel roof over the concourse. There was a gap between the two until after the war but the infilling canopy is scarcely visible. Best of all from the author's point** of view is the sight of the wooden goods shed now much the worse for wear and near the end of its life. The majority of photos taken here have trains at No 2 platform and they conceal the store. No 8 is on the middle road; the train it had brought in may have departed behind another engine. Next out will be bogie tank No 15 on the off-peak 'half-set' in No 3 platform, to the left of the picture. The one jarring note comes from the buses parked in the goods yard. The sidings there appear to have been lifted already.

Above: The second view is in the up direction. The light is beginning to fail; carriages have been placed in the sidings for the night and it is assumed that No 8 has been filling her tanks before going on shed – she was the Bangor engine in the late 1940s. Beyond the 'Boyne Bridge' (carrying Brunswick Road) are silhouetted the engine shed gable and the chimney of its sand drier.

Top: **The scene at Bangor Upper Yard is still predominently vintage BCDR on 11th July 1949 but work is about to begin on a new goods store to replace the old one that is soon to be displaced by the bus station. The facing connection from the up main to the headshunt is in the foreground, with the engine shed out of sight to the left. The advanced starting signal in the distance is a 'sky arm' to enable it to be seen over the Boyne Bridge which is behind the photographer. It is good to have a record of the Bangor home gantry in its complete form, even though it appears to be growing out of No 18's dome. The goods yard home arm will go soon, and the sky arm will be cut down like Lucifer.**

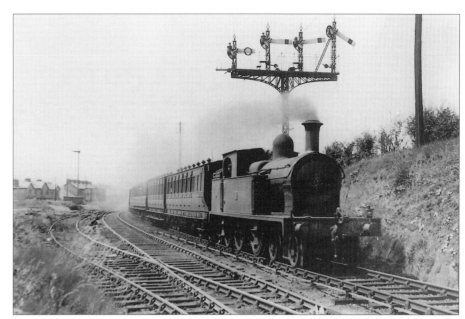

Centre: **One of the larger BCDR cabins, and the last built to the design of G P Culverwell to remain in service, Bangor cabin was closed in April 1988 and demolished in November 1995, at the ripe old age of 97. The catwalk under the windows was a late addition.** C Aspinwall

Bottom: **This is another evening view, taken from the Boyne Bridge on 9th June 1952. The end of steam on the Bangor line is still 15 months away and 'Baltic' tank No 222 is now the occupant of Bangor shed. Engine drivers were among the residents of the railway houses on the Belfast Road in the background – it was like having your garage at the end of the garden! For good measure there is a distant view of the new Bangor goods store on the right. This must be a prime example of how to make railways lose money. Apparently all the freight facilities demolished in the old goods yard were to be reinstated in the Upper Yard; they included the substantial gantry crane shown here, on a new siding. 'A Hornby siding' was the contemptuous comment by Drew Donaldson: its sleepers were widely spaced and it lacked ballast. By the time the new depot was ready, freight services had been withdrawn from the Bangor line. We did hear it suggested that the depot was to be a shared road/rail facility, but we cannot recall any activity around the new building, and it had been sold off by the 1960s.**

LOCOMOTIVES AND ROLLING STOCK

LOCOMOTIVES

By the year 1901 the total locomotive stock had reached 30, and no higher number was carried by a BCDR engine. The number 30 was significant in being given to the first of the 'bogie tanks', which may be regarded as the standard motive power for the rest of the Company's existence, there being 12 almost identical engines plus the three larger 4-4-2Ts, which together made up 50% of the stock. We shall look at the individual types in order of their introduction, bearing in mind that the review covers engines in stock from 1930 onwards. In this period there was one significant change of locomotive livery. From 1920, J L Crosthwait saw fit to modify the elaborate pre-war livery by simplifying the lining-out and substituting rectangular polished steel numberplates for the previous oval brass plates. He also introduced transfer lettering, BCDR, on tank (but not tender) sides, similarly proportioned to carriage lettering but rather larger. Most engines continued to carry a small version of the Company insignia, a combination of the arms of Down and Belfast, with the latter's supporting beasts, above the Company title on a scroll. R G Miller's background colour of 'invisible' green, almost black but with a green cast like spilled oil, was retained. The last engine to be turned out in this livery was the diesel No 28 in 1937, but in the same year a lighter shade of green, we can only describe it as dark olive green, was introduced, and the lining-out was reduced to a scarlet line inside one of white on tank, tender and cab sides, splashers and valancing. Boiler bands continued to be picked out in scarlet inside double white lines. Buffer beams were vermilion, lined in white, with numbers front and rear. Very few engines received the olive green by the outbreak of the war, and judging by the state of others, little repainting had taken place in the 1930s. With wartime prosperity, the new livery was applied to all engines except the diesels and Nos 14 and 28, before the BCDR had been taken over by the UTA.

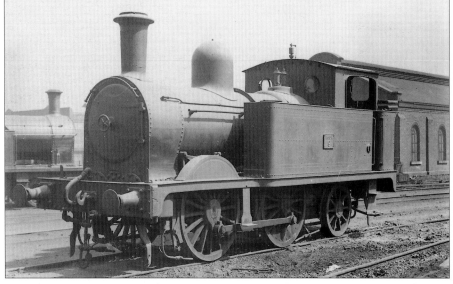

Top left: **No 9, an 0-4-2 tank, was the last survivor of a class of five built by Sharp, Stewart of Manchester as mixed traffic 0-4-2 tender engines. The advent of the 4-4-2Ts rendered them surplus to main line requirements, so Sharp's supplied the components to enable them to be rebuilt as tank engines. They were handy for the sharp curves on the Ardglass harbour tramway and Belfast docks. After 1918, some of the class worked the Holywood 'motors' until worn out. No 9, built in 1887, rebuilt 1900, ended her days as spare shunting engine at Belfast. Seemingly last used in the early 1940s, there were tantalising glimpses of her at the far end of Belfast shed. By 1944 she was out-of-doors at the end of the loco headshunt and on arrival of the new 'big tank' No 9, was given the painted number 28 and hidden in a carriage shed. BCDR accountants apparently insisted on keeping the stock at 30, whether serviceable or not.** H C Casserley

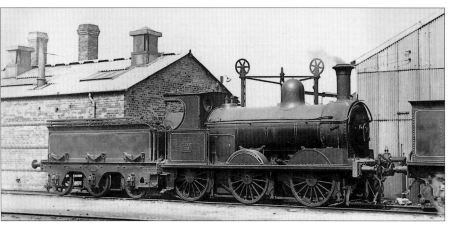

Left: **All the other BCDR steam locomotives illustrated were products of Beyer, Peacock & Company Ltd of Gorton Works, Manchester. No 26 was the third 0-6-0 to be owned by the Company, a typical Beyer workhorse supplied in 1892 and portrayed in front of the gasworks at Queen's Quay on 17th April 1948. She has had a partial repaint and now carries lining, having seen out the Second World War in unlined olive green. Note the polished splasher plate inscribed with makers' name and address, and the building date. Beyers' progressive number (3514) appeared on the oval works plate on the tender side frame.** H C Casserley

Above: **No 26 was re-boilered around 1919 and the cab roof was extended at the same time. Here she makes one of her last outdoor appearances on 14th May 1950; she had not been steamed since the January closure.** H S Brighty

Centre right: **Built in 1894, No 6 was a 'simple' 2-4-0 of similar appearance to the three short-lived Worsdell-Von Borries compounds delivered in 1892. She was re-boilered in 1919 and thereafter was regarded as the spare engine. The tender weatherboard, useful for branch-line working tender first, seems to have been added at rebuilding. She is seen here at Ballynahinch on 16th October 1932.** A W Croughton

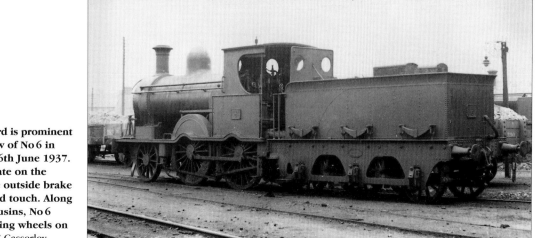

Right: **The tender weatherboard is prominent in this three-quarter rear view of No 6 in Belfast locomotive yard on 26th June 1937. Also visible is the number-plate on the back-sheet of the tender. The outside brake rigging lends an old-fashioned touch. Along with her three compound cousins, No 6 had the largest diameter driving wheels on the County Down, at 6ft.** H C Casserley

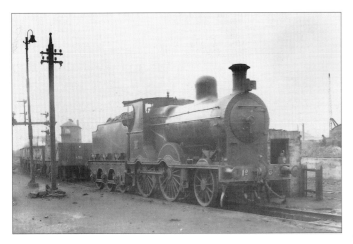

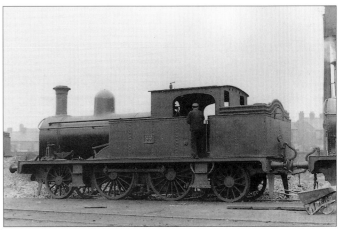

Above, left: **By 1942, No 6 was one of the trio of rusting hulks we looked for as our train passed the back end of Belfast shed. But plans were afoot. In 1943, in the midst of wartime austerity, a wonderful vision was made manifest, a shining, immaculate green 2-4-0: No 6 had been rebuilt with a larger Belpaire boiler, shorter boiler mountings, virtually a new cab without the old square side panels, a new tender tank and side sheets. She returned to main line duties, shedded at Newcastle, and the story of her subsequent career has been outlined earlier in this book. In April 1946 No 6 has been coaled at Queen's Quay and still retains a fair polish.** J G Dewing

Above, right: **Another 2-4-2T, No 27, at the coal stacks on 8th July 1931, was one of four engines, Nos 8, 27, 28 and 29, delivered a year later than Nos 5 and 7 and unaccountably built with smaller tanks, which had a capacity of about 1100 gallons against 1600 gallons on the earlier engines. The weight difference would have been no more than two or three tons. By the 1930s there was little work for all six 2-4-2Ts. By chance, No 27 was the last of the 'short tank' series to survive, and wartime shortage of motive power decreed that she be put in good order and given a pair of full-length side tanks (see bottom photograph, page 44). She was withdrawn in November 1949.** Author's collection

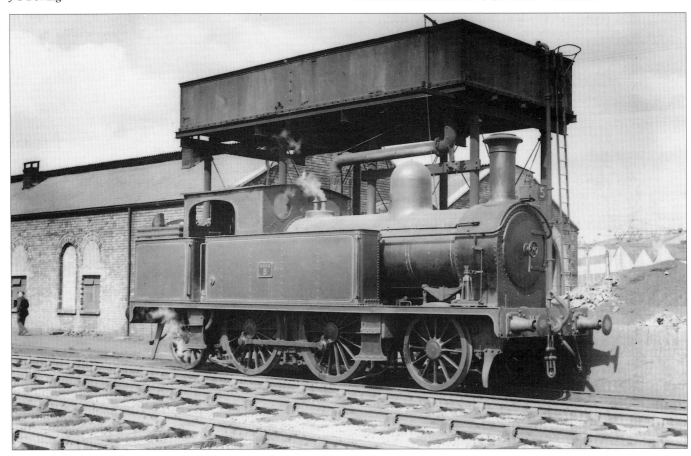

Bottom: **No 5 was a 2-4-2 tank engine built in 1896 for general passenger duties. Outclassed by the 'bogie tanks', like her sister engine No 7, No 5 had a short period on the main line after which both of the** locomotives passed their time mostly employed on branch services and local trains. They were withdrawn by the UTA in November 1949. No 5 is seen at the Queen's Quay water tank on 18th April 1946, not that long after repainting in olive green. J G Dewing

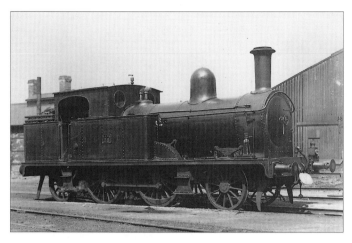

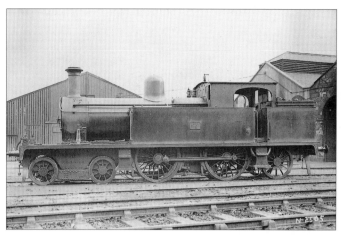

Above left: **As mentioned on page 76, it seems to have been accountancy practices that kept obsolete locomotives from scrap. 0-4-2T No 28 (the former No 9) was photographed in steam on 5th August 1930, but was past further use when replaced by the Harlandic Bo-Bo diesel-electric locomotive, which took her number, in 1937.** H C Casserley

Above right: **The first five of the 'bogie tanks' were subtly different to their younger sisters, having boilers pitched 3in lower than the latter. No 30, the pioneer 4-4-2T of 1901, is now happily resident in the Railway Gallery of the Ulster Folk & Transport Museum at Cultra, though her livery is open to argument. In works order she was followed by Nos 3 and 15, in 1901, and Nos 11 and 12 of 1904. They began life with round-topped fireboxes but all were later re-boilered with Belpaire boxes to match the later engines. Here is No 12 in the 1930s, in unlined green. At top right may be seen part of the clerestory ventilators that ran the length of Belfast running shed; they were removed during the war.** Author's collection

Bottom: **This view of No 30 at the water tank in Belfast locomotive yard is notable in that it shows that the tank fillers on these 4-4-2Ts were at the back and not on the side tanks, which was the more usual arrangement. This view is across the main line at the east end of the engine shed. The 'railmotor' shed is in the right background.** Author's collection

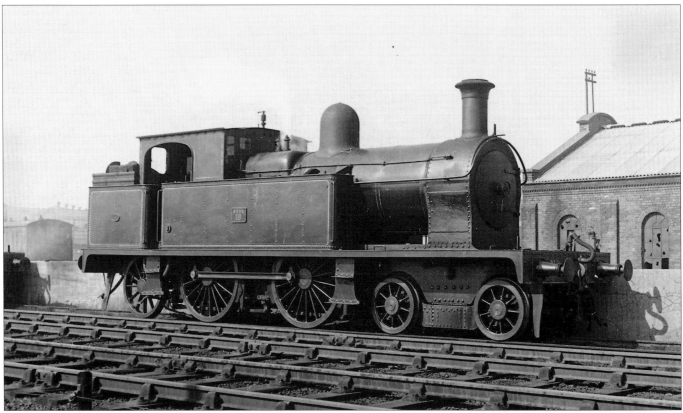

Top: **A rear view of No 11 pulling out of Queen's Quay on 17th April 1948 also gives a good, if distant, view over the yard. The brake coach is No 15, a composite 6-wheeler with two second and two third-class compartments, built in 1905.**
H C Casserley

Above: **The 'bogie tanks' built with Belpaire boilers were Nos 1, 17 and 20 in 1909 and Nos 13, 18, 19 and 21 ordered by J L Crosthwait and delivered in 1921. The last batch was given Cartazzi axle boxes on their trailing wheels, earlier engines had radial trucks. Personal preference when it came to looks was for the last seven engines but all 12 seemed smarter** than the 1892 4-4-2T built by Beyers for the Wirral Railway. **Even so, why did the BCDR wait nearly ten years for its ideal engine when the basic design was there all the time? The Locomotive Committee of the 1890s made some funny decisions. In this picture, No 18 poses at Queen's Quay on 28th March 1948.** E S Russell

Top right: **4-4-2 tank No 13 stands at the coal stacks at Queen's Quay on 17th July 1931. The unfortunate connotations that go with this particular number all but escaped this locomotive except for the occasion one Sunday in 1944 when her driver lost control whilst approaching Bangor, when on a coal train consisting of 13 wagons and a guard's van. The fact that the van, the fourteenth vehicle in the train, was numbered 13, also attracted considerable attention. The engine mounted the buffers of platform No 2 and demolished several bicycles as well as the railings on the concourse. No 13 was soon returned to service – a tribute to the durability of the workmanship of her builders', Beyer Peacock.** A W Croughton

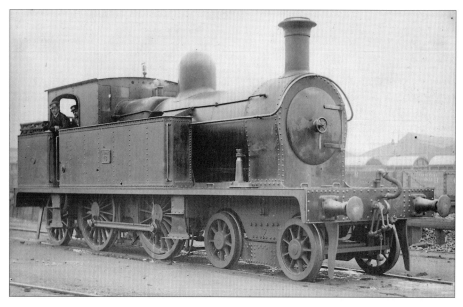

Centre: **Nos 12 and 13 exhibit interesting detail differences in cab design when seen from the rear. They were photographed on 20th June 1938, outside Belfast shed. No 12, on the left, is in the new dark olive green livery, introduced the previous year. Berkeley Wise's extension to Queen's Quay shed, on the left, contrasts with the ashlar masonry of the old BHBR gable, on the right of the picture.** H C Casserley

Bottom: **No 217 was the only BCDR 4-4-2 tank to be given the UTA lined black livery, which actually suited it very well. The locomotive is seen here in 1950 at the former LMS/NCC York Road Station in Belfast. No 217's finest hour came on 24th July 1952 when it was sent out to rescue the prototype six-car diesel railcar set which had failed at Craigavad, disrupting the evening rush hour in the process.** Author's collection

Above: **The first No 14 was a very successful 0-6-0 built by the Vulcan Foundry in 1875. In 1904 the Vulcan was replaced by another 0-6-0, Beyers' price being £2,587 for engine only. The old tender frames were retained and fitted with a new 2,000 gallon tank supplied by Vulcan. No 14 seems to have been a magnet for most photographers and has already figured in** this book. **This illustration, at Queen's Quay locomotive yard on 26th March 1946, shows her with a headlamp fronted by a stencil bearing her number. We have never come across a satisfactory explanation for this other than it was to have been in connection with some form of train control. A few other engines had the device, including No 6, but it did not last long.**

Below: **This Henry Casserley view, taken on 5th August 1930, is a classic. It shows No 14 on a main line departure from the Belfast terminus and also emphasises how useful the tender engines were in the summer peak season.**

Top: **The much photographed No 14 is seen at Queen's Quay in the early 1930s. Though the locomotive was a product of Beyer Peacock, it was coupled to a tender originally built by the Vulcan Foundry for an earlier No 14 dating from 1875 and renewed when this locomotive was built in 1904.** Author's collection

Centre right: **With three 0-6-0s on the books, the need was felt for a fourth, and R G Miller recommended scrapping 0-4-2T No 10 to make room for it. He had tried vainly to have old No 10 rebuilt as a 0-6-0 tank to act as Belfast yard shunter. The new No 10 was delivered in 1914, an impressive-looking beast with a boiler of almost 4ft 11in diameter. The tender had particularly clean lines and was the first on the BCDR to have the bearing springs placed below the running plate, allowing for a full-width water tank. In this Newcastle view, No 10 has arrived with an excursion, complete with 6-wheel saloon next the engine.** Drew Donaldson

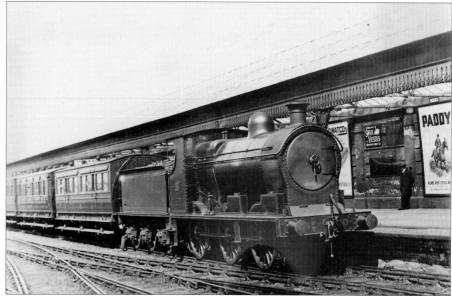

Bottom right: **When the previous No 4, a Beyer 0-6-0 of 1878, was worn out, she was replaced in 1921 by another large 0-6-0 to the same design as No 10. This engine-only view of No 4 shows a wealth of detail. The date is 5th August 1930.** H C Casserley

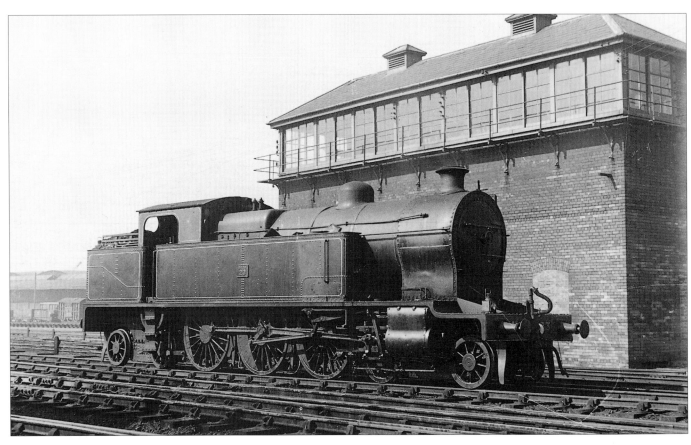

Above: **Legendary is probably a good adjective with which to describe the four Baltic 4-6-4 tank locomotives, for many years the largest tank engines in Ireland, that landed on John L Crosthwait's plate almost as soon as he took office in 1920. No other County Down engines generated so much mythology as those handsome but so disappointing products of Gorton Works. The first order to Beyer Peacock in 1915 was for two inside-cylindered 'mixed traffic' 2-6-4 tank engines. With the contemporary need for increased motive** power on the Bangor line, the mixed-traffic notion was completely obscured by G P Culverwell's advocacy of engines with a symmetrical wheel arrangement, 'the 4-6-4 is the perfection of the tank type'. For Beyers, it was literally 'back to the drawing board'. An order for four 4-6-4Ts with 5ft 6in coupled wheels and 19in x 26in outside cylinders was placed in 1918 and the engines, Nos 22-25, were delivered in mid-1920. Careful analysis by the late Bob Clements of available evidence led him to conclude that Beyer, Peacock's draughts-man, designing to the client's deadline and constantly hampered by new suggestions from Culverwell (not Miller, whose resignation had been proffered), became thoroughly fed-up with a thankless task. The result was four beautiful coal-devouring monsters that flattered to deceive. Their performance is exemplified by an incident with No 25 on 29th November 1943. She got stuck on Holywood bank with the down Bangor goods consisting of only 24 laden wagons and a van, and had to be pushed to Bangor by the engine of the 5.55am train, which was still coupled to its coaches whilst performing the rescue! E S Russell's study of No 23 in front of Belfast Home Cabin on 28th March 1948 reinforces what has been said about Beyer, Peacock & Company and locomotive aesthetics.

Left: **We had been accustomed to seeing No 29 from street level and certain features became more apparent from higher up, including the twin headlamps on the bunker as well as on the front buffer beam. As 229, she waits at the Harbour gate on 13th May 1950.** H S Brighty

Above: **Elegant to the end, Baltic No 223 awaits its appointment with the cutter's torch at the back end of Queen's Quay yard on 20th June 1955. By this time the Bangor Branch was entirely worked by diesel railcars, one of the first lines in the British Isles to succumb to the onward march of diesel traction.** Peter W Gray

Below: **From 1908, R G Miller had been aware and no doubt envious of the Great Northern RT class 0-6-4T, purpose-built for shunting on Belfast's quays, that crossed BCDR metals daily. The need for a proper yard shunter became acute when the temporary expedient, 0-6-0 No 26, broke down in 1919. An 0-6-4 tank, No 29, inspired by** the GNR design, was eventually delivered in September 1923. The NCC never had a suitable steam engine for its side of the harbour. After 30 years on the County Down quays No 229, as it became, was snapped up by York Road and ended its useful life there in 1955. This view shows No 29 at Queen's Quay on 6th June 1949. E S Russell

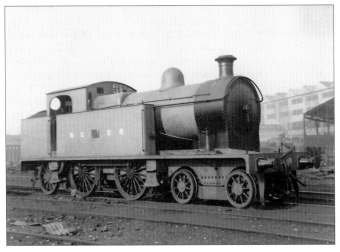

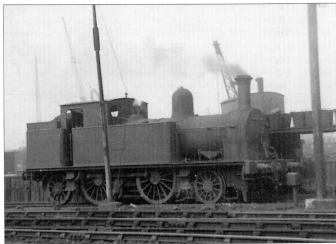

Top: **J L Crosthwait was permitted to replace two of the small engines in 1924 and wisely chose a larger version of the 4-4-2T type. Nos 8 and 16 were not allowed on the Bangor line until the following year. They were then hampered with the restricted axle loading mentioned in the introduction. Thus was their potential wasted for several years. Here is No 8, in the old livery, on Belfast turntable, 5th August 1930.**
H C Casserley

Lower left: **The 4-4-2 tank No 9 was the last locomotive delivered to the BCDR. Though the official building date of No 9 was 1944,** the engine was assembled at Queen's Quay in the first weeks of 1945. On 9th February word came that she was in steam. When we got to the shed her fire had been dropped and she was indoors. Fortunately, Driver Paddy Fitzpatrick was able to bring her back into daylight on the residual steam pressure. No 9 is seen in her shop grey, with white initials. Number plates had been taken from the old 0-4-2T and were still very rusty. Driver Fitzpatrick swore by No 9 and insisted on doing his own valve-setting when she was in the shop. He shared her with another senior driver, John Heyburn. With the arrival of WT 2-6-4T No 53, Paddy found he had an even better engine.

He finished his driving career on the DMUs, pleased to be able to sit down and smoke his pipe behind glass.

Lower right: **The hired Great Southern engine No 430, seemingly a shy creature, was photographed at the Belfast coal stacks in March 1944. Her eventual return south went unrecorded. Built by the Dublin Wicklow & Wexford Railway as their No 11 in 1896, No 430 was seen again at her old haunt, Grand Canal Street shed on the Westland row line, in 1950. By then Inchicore works had given her a Belpaire boiler, though she did not last long in this condition, being withdrawn in 1952.**

Above: **The diesel-electric locomotive, numbered D1 on the BCDR, was the first of an unfortunately short run of these machines turned out at Harland & Wolff's Belfast shipyard. H&W were making a name for themselves with marine diesel engines, but there were many problems in designing engines for railway working and D1 was very much a pioneer. She had a six-wheeled rigid frame with traction motors on the centre and rear axles. A conventional cab at the rear and exhaust at the front in the form of a steam locomotive chimney were perhaps a gesture to tradition. D1 was renumbered 2 in 1937 and up to then had been the 31st engine on the BCDR list. She spent all her chequered career on the Ballynahinch branch until its closure, when** with her two coaches she was dispatched to Newcastle, the lawyers having found that the UTA were obliged still to have a nominal presence on the Castlewellan extension. A way out of this was found in 1951 and No 2 was returned to Harland & Wolff, finishing her days as a works shunter. William Robb's photograph shows her almost new as D1 at Comber on 15th July 1933.

Bottom left and right: **By happy coincidence, Henry Casserley visited Queen's Quay on 26th June 1937 and found the Bo-Bo diesel-electric locomotive No 28 resplendent in what was to have been her first and last application of County Down livery. No 28 is seen** outside the former railmotor shed that provided a useful domicile when she was on test. A diesel for the Ardglass branch was mooted in 1934, Harland & Wolff were keenly interested in the project and offered deferred payments. After much delay, delivery took place on 11th May 1937. A satisfactory trial run was made to Bangor and back that month, and what was to have been regular work on the Ardglass branch began on 8th September. There followed seven years of trouble until No 28 was returned to the makers in December 1944. No 28 did eventually have the distinction of being the last BCDR locomotive to remain in service. She ended her days as yard shunter at Great Victoria Street, in the 1960s. Both photographs by H C Casserley

SIX WHEEL CARRIAGES

Top: **In the 1880s, County Down passenger stock was a by-word for decrepitude, with the BHBR a close runner-up. Joseph Tatlow persuaded his board to start ordering new coaches. Six-wheel third No 105, seen in an excursion rake at Newcastle on 9th July 1949, was one of a batch built by the Railway Carriage Company of Oldbury in 1888. This five-compartment coach was second class when delivered; the 'rounded sides' and a tumblehome below the waist, costing an extra £5 per coach. The thirds proper had uncompromisingly vertical sides, and have been glimpsed previously on excursion trains in this volume.**

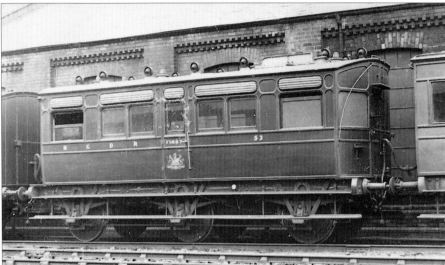

Left and below: **Tatlow also convinced the directors that they needed a 'State Carriage' and the Metropolitan Carriage & Wagon Company of Birmingham supplied this charming but dated coupé-ended 6-wheel saloon in 1889. No 53 was known as the 'Royal Saloon' by Queen's Quay men, though we have no evidence for its use as such. Some time in middle life it was given a lavatory at one end, and Henry Casserley's picture (left) taken on 26th June 1937 shows it thus. In 1939 the lavatory was removed and the author recalls No 53 stationed at Bangor during the war as one of the saloons used by card-playing commuters on the business trains. Rather shaky by then, it was marshalled next the engine. In its final condition, and not long after repainting, No 53 was photographed by H S Brighty.**

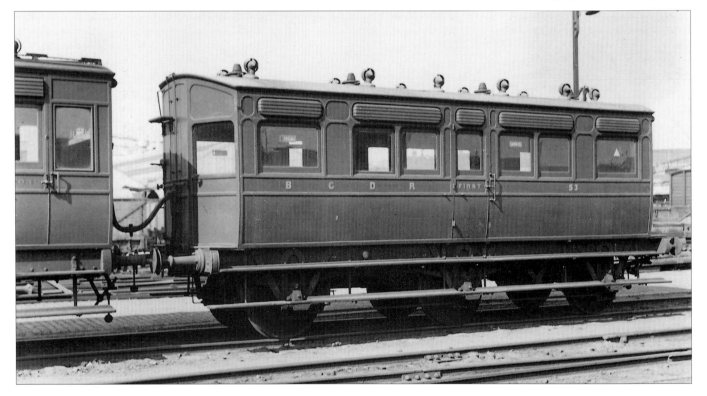

Top right: **The coach nearest the camera is No 137, a brake composite accommodating first and second class passengers. One of two built by the Ashbury Railway Carriage & Iron Company of Manchester in 1893, non-standard designs like this were found in branch sets and as spares. The vehicle to the right of No 137 is a 6-wheel passenger brake (second series) similar to that illustrated on page 93 but built by the Metropolitan Carriage & Wagon Company with more conventional BCDR panelling and retaining the straight sides.** H S Brighty

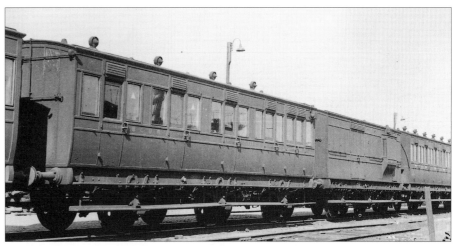

Centre: **Most numerous of the County Down 6-wheelers were the 6-compartment seconds; 41 were built from 1905 to 1921, later examples having Stones' electric light. No 34 of 1921, is seen freshly-painted in BCDR crimson at Bangor in 1949. The Ulster Transport Authority was a long time deciding on its livery for locomotives and rolling stock, and Harold Houston had to keep his painters busy...**

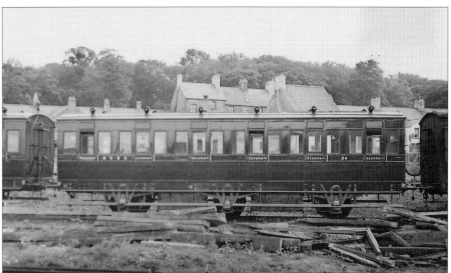

Below: **Queen's Quay turned out three first class saloons, Nos 2, 3 and 4 in 1916. There had been a long-standing tradition of saloon accommodation on the BHBR and the last of the old stock had been scrapped. Nos 2 and 4 were downgraded to second class just before the Second World War though they reverted to firsts on the Downpatrick Race Days. With seating along the sides and passengers' backs to the windows, they were not popular but appeared regularly in the summer. Here is No 4, still first class, on 26th June 1937.** H C Casserley

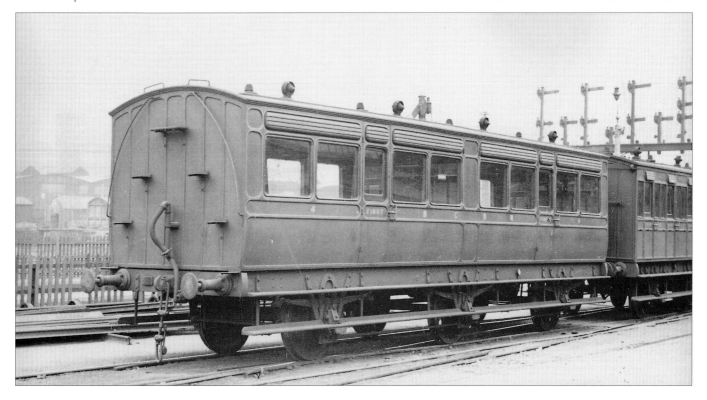

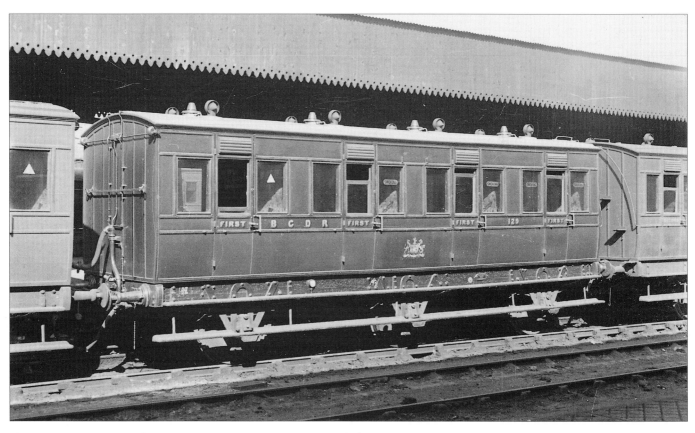

Above: **Four-compartment first class 6-wheelers were distributed through Bangor line sets. Ten of these, Nos 120 to 129, were built by Ashbury in 1891, though two were eventually down-graded to third class.** E S Russell

Below: **Many BCDR bogie coaches, along with the 1920s-built 6-wheelers, were retained for excursion traffic on the NCC sections until the early 1960s. Their last resting place was the former GNR yard at Adelaide, Belfast, which also became a vast graveyard for UTA wagon stock.**

As can be seen, it is doubtful if any of these coaches had received Brunswick Green more than once during UTA ownership. The partially visible 6-wheeler on the right is a second; next to it are two of the seven-compartment thirds and one of the former railmotors. David Anderson

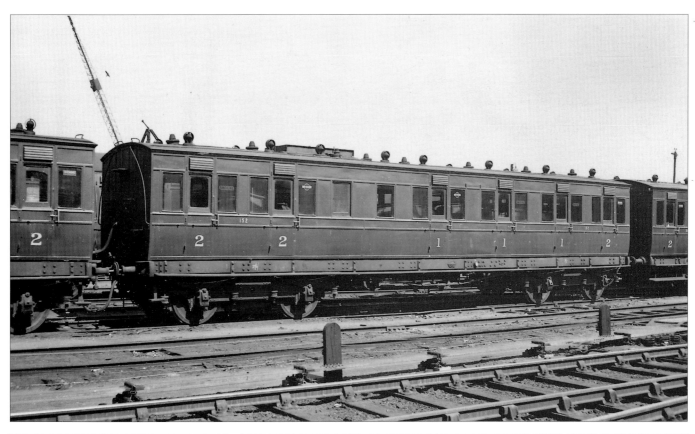

BOGIE CARRIAGES

Top: **Two of the bogie composites were given lavatory accommodation in the 1920s. One worked to Castlewellan and the other to Donaghadee. No 152 is at Belfast on 27th April 1951. The low roof profile required the use of external water tanks. One second class and half a first class compartment were sacrificed for the two lavatories.**

Centre: **The Ashbury Company provided the BCDR's first dozen bogie carriages in 1897. Six of them were first-second composites, mostly used on main line trains. Once 'Brunswick green' had been chosen as the UTA carriage livery the bogie stock was repainted quickly; seen here is No 149 at Newcastle on 9th July 1949.**

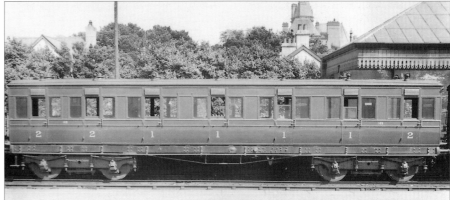

Bottom: **The Ashbury bogie brake-thirds were built with eight compartments. No 146 was one of two to lose a compartment for extra luggage space but remained unique in having its side panelling modified. No 144 just had the doors screwed up. They were used on an all-bogie main line set during the post-war decline, along with the two tri-composites of 1938. The UTA enlarged the vans of the remaining four in a similar fashion.**

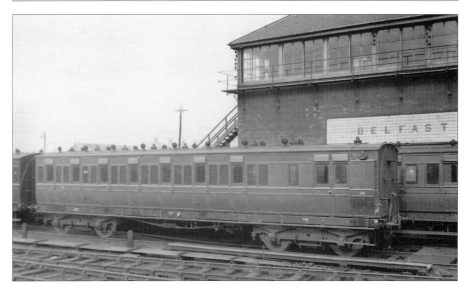

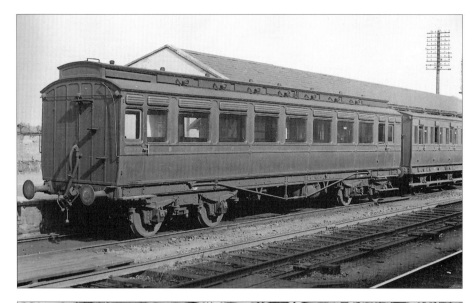

Top: **Three steam railmotors, Nos 1 to 3, were acquired for Belfast to Holywood and Belfast to Dundonald suburban services in 1905-6. Kitson & Company built the power units, similar to those for the English Great Northern though differently styled. The bodies were supplied by the Metropolitan Carriage & Wagon Company. The engines were worn out by 1918 and the carriage portions converted for push-pull working. This practice was abandoned after the fatal accident at Ballymacarrett in January 1945, the 'Holywood Motors' being renumbered into the carriage list as Nos 59, 72 and 173. The former driving compartment was retained for guard's use. No 59 is pictured at Comber on 6th June 1949. Within a few weeks it was painted Brunswick green, a most depressing colour for coaches, wiping out the individual character created by various styles of panelling.** E S Russell

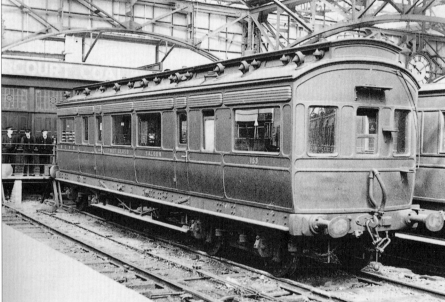

Centre: **A glorious example of Victorian exuberance. The 1897 Royal Saloon took on a new lease of life in the 1920s when it became what the Manager prosaically described as a 'working carriage'. The only noticeable external alteration was to provide an additional door on each side. Internally, the three saloons were given fixed seating each side, with drop-leaf tables (the mixture as before). There was a separate lavatory and washroom, no doubt furnished much less exotically than before. The original Ashbury creation had cost the BCDR upwards of £1,400 but was good publicity. No 153 normally spent weekdays against the buffers at Queen's Quay, well protected from the elements, and this was where Eric Russell took the finest photograph of the saloon known to the author. It is June 1949, and the crimson lake paint and gold-leaf lettering will be obliterated in a few weeks time.**

Bottom: **Very much strapped for cash, it is to the Company's credit that it made the effort to purchase two splendid tri-composite bogie coaches in 1938. Working drawings were produced in the NCC drawing office at York Road, using a standard LMS underframe design. R Y Pickering of Glasgow built the pair, BCDR Nos 120 and 121. Their riding qualities were noticeably smoother than LMS-built coaches. With money coming in from increased traffic, the BCDR tried to get a couple more, but was refused government permission. No 120 was photographed on 26th February 1951.**

VANS

Top: **Nine 6-wheel passenger brake vans to the same general design were on the books from the 1890s. The first few came from the Railway Carriage Company and matched their 1888 coaches. Originally numbered 1 to 9, they were brought into the main passenger list in 1945. This is No 190 photographed in 1949.**

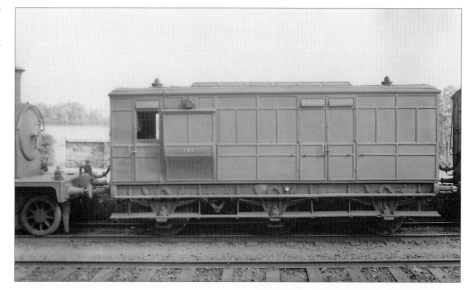

Centre: **The oldest horseboxes on the BCDR list were rather uncommon vehicles, being a double horsebox on six wheels, built in 1890 with the hunting fraternity in mind. By the 1930s there was a clause in the Appendix to the Working Timetable forbidding them to leave the Company's metals, and they remained unknown to most enthusiasts until 1945. Nos 7 and 8 emerged from the 'Vinery' to receive their new numbers, 197 and 198, and spent the rest of their existence slowly decaying out-of-doors at Queen's Quay. They had been the first non-passenger coaching vehicles to be given the crimson livery, but it had weathered to a sort of pink by April 1951, when No 197 was photographed. The remaining 4-wheeled horseboxes, well-built and useful, were retained by the UTA for several more years in preference to the LMS horseboxes.**

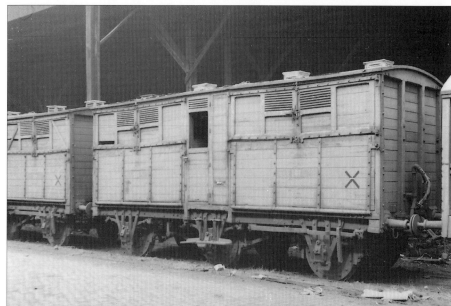

Bottom: **The 6-wheeled fish vans were intended for the Ardglass herring traffic. Nos 1 and 2 were built in 1911 while 3 and 4 followed in 1917. Ardglass fish traffic declined and the four vans were pressed into service as bread vans: cleaning them cannot have been an easy task! Despite that, the inscription FISH VAN appeared on each until someone in the UTA saw the anomaly. All four had 200 added to their numbers in 1945. The last two were a couple of inches higher from floor to cantrail than Nos 1 and 2, as is borne out by this view of 202 taken on 1st April 1951; the van on the left is either 203 or 204. By then all were in Brunswick green with yellow writing. The crosses marking them out for scrapping were premature. All four were sent to the NCC section when the mistake was discovered and they joined very similar LMS vans on parcels trains.**

GOODS WAGONS

Ordinary unfitted goods wagons on the BCDR were painted a very dark grey. Vacuum-braked and piped stock, mostly of the 'goods and cattle type' were painted a bauxite red or red oxide colour; this was also applied to the permanent way wagons, including the PW brakevan No 173 and the breakdown van. Ironwork, including axleguards and brake gear below solebar level, was painted black. Wagon 'writing', as the signwriters termed it, was stencilled in white, the company initials and numerals were in a distinctive style. A striking feature of all rigid wheelbase vehicles, passenger or goods, was the use of outside axleguards, a practice going back to the earliest days of the railway age.

Top: The goods and cattle wagons were of a type widely used on Irish railways in the nineteenth century. No 47 was one of 45 vacuum braked examples, distinguished by a star over the number. There were a further 34 with through pipes. All had buffers and drawgear to passenger standards, and oil axleboxes. Another 40 of the type were confined to goods trains. No 47 was photographed on 10th April 1951.

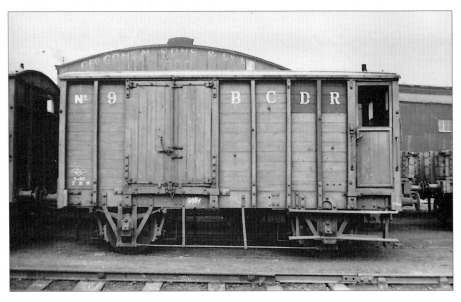

Centre: Covered wagon No 397, built in 1911, was one of 174 8- and 10-ton wagons of more conventional design; the type first appeared early this century. Recorded on 12th January 1950, it stands at the old Ballygowan cattle beach, partly on the miniscule catch siding, that because of limited clearance was provided with half a buffer stop.

Bottom: All 14 BCDR goods brake vans were of this totally enclosed design of the 1890s, though three vans including No 9 shown here on 1st March 1950, had one extra stanchion between the double doors and the guard's door. Tare weight had been seven tons originally but some vans were being renewed as 12-tonners. Nine 7-ton vans remained in 1948.

Top: **The design of this 8-ton open wagon dates from the 1880s and though a 10-ton version was mass-produced from 1891, 8-tonners continued to be built or renewed until the last years. When handed over, there were 229 10-ton wagons in stock and 35 8-tonners. As will be seen from this photograph of 1961, BCDR wagons have had 6000 added to their numbers. Initials were obliterated in grey paint that soon washed off, revealing the good standard of workmanship in the Queen's Quay paint shops.**

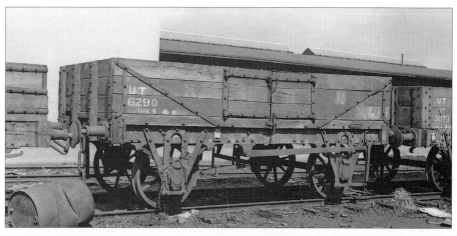

Second from top: **In 1890, a dozen 16-ton 6-wheel ballast wagons were built at York Road by the BNCR at cost price for the BCDR. Relations must have been good between the two companies at that time! The wagons saw intensive use and were renewed at Queen's Quay over the years. Some, like No 388 seen here, had vertical screw handbrakes and a hutch for the brakesman. When Drumhirk ballast quarry closed in the 1930s, the hutches were ordered to be removed. They had been retained for their ability to pass under the screening plant. Three hutch wagons survived to become UTA stock.**

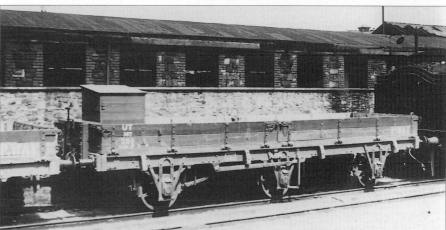

Third from top: **There were also 12 more conventional ballast wagons of 6- and 8-ton capacity. No 133 is illustrated at the old Queen's Quay cattle beach, which became a permanent way siding when cattle traffic ceased. For a time these PW wagons were painted in an attractive but short-lived two-tone scheme that was introduced at Queen's Quay in 1950; the top plank was bauxite red and the remainder of the vehicle in NCC wagon grey. 'P.WAY' was in BCDR stencilling.**

Bottom: **UTA No 6417 is an example of J L Crosthwait's rail wagons of 1923. These were a heavier version of the single-bolster timber trucks, running on oil axleboxes and having the wings of the outside axle guards turned vertically against the solebar.**

Top: **In the days when every goods yard had its cart weighbridge, these appliances had to be checked and tested periodically. The Weighbridge Van was a mobile workshop, carrying fitters' equipment from place to place, marshalled in a pick-up goods train. The BCDR van, painted wagon grey, was un-numbered and each side was different, one had a pair of double doors. Photographed on 26th March 1946, the side we are looking at hints at the vehicle having been a ballast brake before that. It also bore notices 'Not to be loose shunted or loose shunted against', plus it had a skylight in the roof, and a stovepipe chimney.**

Centre: **The two gasholder trucks were also without numbers and did not figure in the stock returns, being classed as 'plant'. They were branded BALLYNAHINCH and DOWN-PATRICK, where they were kept to supply oil-gas to the coaches in the branch sets. Here they await their fate in a remote corner of Queen's Quay yard on 10th April 1951.**

Bottom: **Private owners wagons were a feature of the Ballygowan and Scrabo quarries. Charles Ritchie & Sons were comparative newcomers at Ballygowan, opening a siding in December 1891. Hurst Nelson & Company of Motherwell supplied eight stone wagons to Ritchies in 1896. The works photograph shows them to be typical two-plank dropside 8-ton wagons. Apart from the inside axleguards, an interesting feature is the vertical screw handbrake at one end. This was a BCDR tradition. The only braked vehicles in the original County Down wagon fleet were a handful of 'stone wagons' and it may be assumed that the stone trains, working independently for many years, ran without conventional brake vans. Hence the evolution of brakesmens' hutches. Ritchies had the Bloomfield stone yard referred to previously. The firm failed in 1906 and the BCDR bought their wagons at the bargain price of £96. They were numbered 642 to 649 and used as ballast wagons.**
Author's collection